CONFIGURING PRODUCT INFORMATION MANAGEMENT WITHIN DYNAMICS 365 FOR FINANCE & OPERATIONS

MODULE 2: **CONFIGURING PRODUCTS & SERVICES**

MURRAY FIFE

ISBN-13: 978-1078098243

Preface

What You Need for this Guide

All the examples shown in this blueprint were done with the Microsoft Dynamics 365 for Operations hosted image that was provisioned through Lifecycle Services.

The following list of software from the virtual image was leveraged within this guide:

Microsoft Dynamics 365 for Operations

Even though all the preceding software was used during the development and testing of the recipes in this book, they should also work on later versions without any changes.

Errata

Although we have taken every care to ensure the accuracy of our content, mistakes do happen. If you find a mistake in one of our books—may be a mistake in the text or the code—we would be grateful if you would report this to us. By doing so, you can save other readers from frustration and help us improve subsequent versions of this book. If you find any errata, please report them by emailing editor@dynamicscompanions.com.

Piracy

Piracy of copyright material on the Internet is an ongoing problem across all media. If you come across any illegal copies of our works, in any form, on the Internet, please provide us with the location address or website name immediately so that we can pursue a remedy.

Please contact us at legal@dynamicscompanions.com with a link to the suspected pirated material.

We appreciate your help in protecting our authors and our ability to bring you valuable content.

Questions

You can contact us at help@dynamicscompanions.com if you are having a problem with any aspect of the book, and we will do our best to address it.

Table of Contents

DYNAMICS COMPANIONS
BARE BONES CONFIGURATION GUIDE

CONFIGURING PRODUCT INFORMATION MANAGEMENT WITHIN DYNAMICS 365 FOR FINANCE & OPERATIONS
MODULE 2: CONFIGURING PRODUCTS & SERVICES

Configuring Products & Services

Now that you have all of the basic codes and controls configured you can start adding some real products and services into the Product Information Management area.

In this chapter we will show you how you can set up products and services, and also how you can load in all of your products in bulk through the Data Import Export Framework.

Topics Covered

- Creating New Products

- Creating A Service Item

- Creating Product Templates

DYNAMICS COMPANIONS
BARE BONES CONFIGURATION GUIDE

CONFIGURING PRODUCT INFORMATION MANAGEMENT WITHIN DYNAMICS 365 FOR FINANCE & OPERATIONS
MODULE 2: CONFIGURING PRODUCTS & SERVICES

Creating New Products

Now we can start creating our products. There are a number of different product types that you can configure based on if it is a physical product or a service item, if the product is a simple product or a includes additional configurations and dimensions, and even if the product is configurable based on rules.

In this first example we will start off by creating some simple inventoried items.

Topics Covered

- Opening the Released products form

- Creating a new Product

- Manually Updating Product Details

- Adding A Product Image

- Importing Products Using The Data Import Export Framework

- Summary

DYNAMICS COMPANIONS
BARE BONES CONFIGURATION GUIDE

CONFIGURING PRODUCT INFORMATION MANAGEMENT WITHIN DYNAMICS 365 FOR FINANCE & OPERATIONS
MODULE 2: CONFIGURING PRODUCTS & SERVICES

Opening the Released products form

To do this we will want to open the **Released products** maintenance form which will allow us to configure all of our products that we will be using within the system.

How to do it...

Step 1: Open the Released products form through the menu

We can get to the **Released products** form a couple of different ways. The first way is through the master menu.

Navigate to Product information management > Products > Released products

Step 2: Open the Released Products form through the menu search

Another way that we can find the **Released Products** form is through the menu search feature.

Type in **released products** into the menu search and select **Released Products**

This will open up the **Released products** maintenance form where we will be able to create our new product records.

DYNAMICS COMPANIONS
BARE BONES CONFIGURATION GUIDE

CONFIGURING PRODUCT INFORMATION MANAGEMENT WITHIN DYNAMICS 365 FOR FINANCE & OPERATIONS
MODULE 2: CONFIGURING PRODUCTS & SERVICES

Opening the Released products form

How to do it...

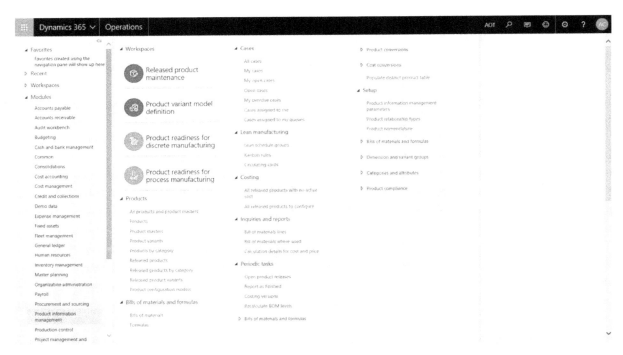

Step 1: Open the Released products form through the menu

We can get to the **Released products** form a couple of different ways. The first way is through the master menu.

To do this, open up the navigation panel, expand out the **Modules** and group, and click on **Product information management** to see all of the menu items that are available. Then click on the **Released products** menu item within the **Products** group.

www.dynamicscompanions.com
Dynamics Companions

- 10 -

www.blindsquirrelpublishing.com
© 2019 Blind Squirrel Publishing, LLC , All Rights Reserved

BLIND SQUIRREL
PUBLISHING

DYNAMICS COMPANIONS
BARE BONES CONFIGURATION GUIDE

CONFIGURING PRODUCT INFORMATION MANAGEMENT WITHIN DYNAMICS 365 FOR FINANCE & OPERATIONS
MODULE 2: CONFIGURING PRODUCTS & SERVICES

Opening the Released products form

How to do it...

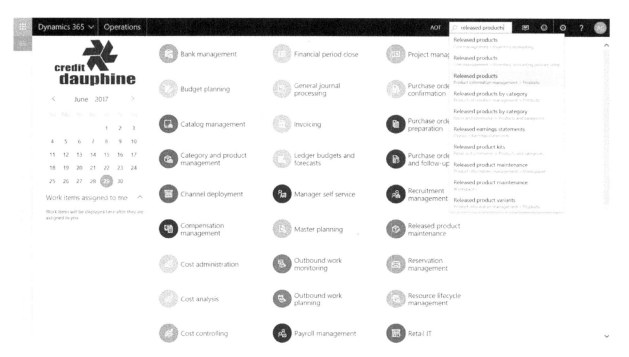

Step 2: Open the Released Products form through the menu search

Another way that we can find the **Released Products** form is through the menu search feature.

We can do this by clicking on the search icon in the header of the form (or by pressing **ALT+G**) and then type in **released products** storage into the search box. Then you will be able to select the **Released Products** form from the dropdown list.

www.dynamicscompanions.com
Dynamics Companions

- 11 -

www.blindsquirrelpublishing.com
© 2019 Blind Squirrel Publishing, LLC , All Rights Reserved

BLIND SQUIRREL
PUBLISHING

DYNAMICS COMPANIONS
BARE BONES CONFIGURATION GUIDE

CONFIGURING PRODUCT INFORMATION MANAGEMENT WITHIN DYNAMICS 365 FOR FINANCE & OPERATIONS
MODULE 2: CONFIGURING PRODUCTS & SERVICES

Opening the Released products form

How to do it...

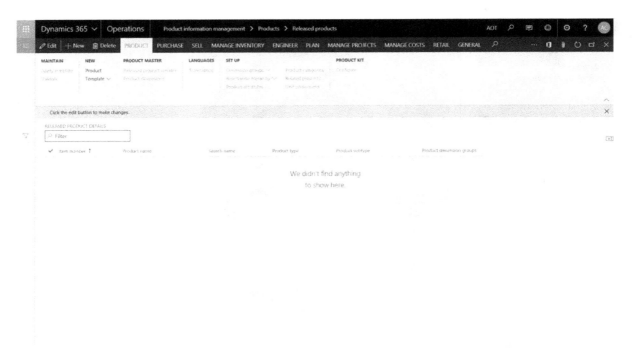

Step 2: Open the Released Products form through the menu search

This will open up the **Released products** maintenance form where we will be able to create our new product records.

www.dynamicscompanions.com
Dynamics Companions

- 12 -

www.blindsquirrelpublishing.com
© 2019 Blind Squirrel Publishing, LLC , All Rights Reserved

BLIND SQUIRREL
PUBLISHING

DYNAMICS COMPANIONS
BARE BONES CONFIGURATION GUIDE

CONFIGURING PRODUCT INFORMATION MANAGEMENT WITHIN DYNAMICS 365 FOR FINANCE & OPERATIONS
MODULE 2: CONFIGURING PRODUCTS & SERVICES

Creating a new Product

Now we can start creating our products. There are a number of different product types that you can configure based on if it is a physical product or a service item, if the product is a simple product or a includes additional configurations and dimensions, and even if the product is configurable based on rules.

How to do it...

Step 1: Click Product

In this first example we will start off by creating a simple inventoried item.

Click on the **Product** button within the **New** group of the **Product** ribbon bar.

This will open up the **New Released Product** creation dialog box.

Step 2: Update the Product number

Set the Product number to 0050209O

Notice that the company specific **Item number** will default in based off the **Product Number**.

Step 3: Update the Product name

Next we will want to add a more descriptive **Product name** for those of us that don't want to decipher product codes all of the time.

Set the Product name to Honeywell 005-02044-0029+O Encoder

Step 4: Update the Search name

Set the Search name to 005-02044-0029+O

Step 5: Select the Storage dimension group

New we will want to change the **Storage Dimension Group** so that we can track this product within our warehouse locations.

Click on the **Storage dimension group** dropdown list and select **LOC**

Step 6: Select the Tracking dimension group

Next we will want to select the **Tracking Dimension Group** to no tacking since we will not be using batch or serial number tracking on this item.

Click on the **Tracking dimension group** dropdown list and select **NONE**

Step 7: Select the Inventory unit

Now we will want to specify the unit of measure that we want to track our inventory quantities in.

Click on the **Inventory unit** dropdown list and select **ea**

www.dynamicscompanions.com
Dynamics Companions

- 13 -

www.blindsquirrelpublishing.com
© 2019 Blind Squirrel Publishing, LLC , All Rights Reserved

BLIND SQUIRREL
PUBLISHING

DYNAMICS COMPANIONS
BARE BONES CONFIGURATION GUIDE

CONFIGURING PRODUCT INFORMATION MANAGEMENT WITHIN DYNAMICS 365 FOR FINANCE & OPERATIONS
MODULE 2: CONFIGURING PRODUCTS & SERVICES

Step 8: Select the Purchase unit

Next we will want to choose the unit of measure that we want to track our purchase quantities in.

Click on the **Purchase unit** dropdown list and select **ea**

Step 9: Select the Sales unit

Now we will want to select the unit of measure that we want to track our sales quantities in.

Click on the **Sales unit** dropdown list and select **ea**

Step 10: Click OK

Now we have specified all of the main configuration fields for the product we can create the record.

Click on the **OK** button.

This will take us to the new **Released product** record maintenance form where we will be able to see all of the details of the product.

DYNAMICS COMPANIONS
BARE BONES CONFIGURATION GUIDE

CONFIGURING PRODUCT INFORMATION MANAGEMENT WITHIN DYNAMICS 365 FOR FINANCE & OPERATIONS
MODULE 2: CONFIGURING PRODUCTS & SERVICES

Creating a new Product

How to do it...

Step 1: Click Product

In this first example we will start off by creating a simple inventoried item.

To do this just click on the **Product** button within the **New** group of the **Product** ribbon bar.

www.dynamicscompanions.com
Dynamics Companions

- 15 -

www.blindsquirrelpublishing.com
© 2019 Blind Squirrel Publishing, LLC , All Rights Reserved

BLIND SQUIRREL
PUBLISHING

DYNAMICS COMPANIONS
BARE BONES CONFIGURATION GUIDE

CONFIGURING PRODUCT INFORMATION MANAGEMENT WITHIN DYNAMICS 365 FOR FINANCE & OPERATIONS
MODULE 2: CONFIGURING PRODUCTS & SERVICES

Creating a new Product

How to do it...

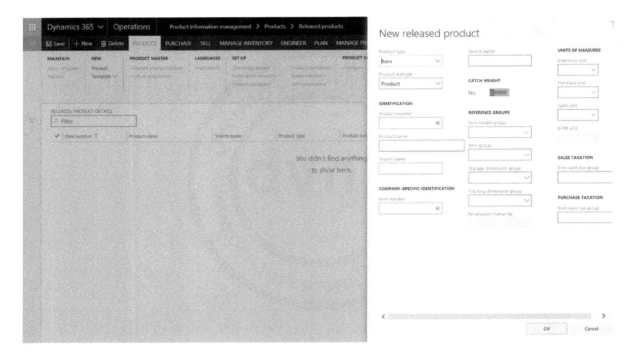

Step 1: Click Product

This will open up the **New Released Product** creation dialog box.

dyn c

www.dynamicscompanions.com
Dynamics Companions

- 16 -

www.blindsquirrelpublishing.com
© 2019 Blind Squirrel Publishing, LLC , All Rights Reserved

BLIND SQUIRREL
PUBLISHING

DYNAMICS COMPANIONS
BARE BONES CONFIGURATION GUIDE

CONFIGURING PRODUCT INFORMATION MANAGEMENT WITHIN DYNAMICS 365 FOR FINANCE & OPERATIONS
MODULE 2: CONFIGURING PRODUCTS & SERVICES

Creating a new Product

How to do it...

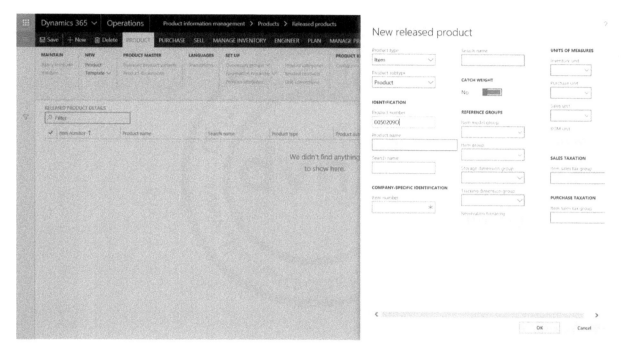

Step 2: Update the Product number

To do this we will just need to update the **Product number** value.

For this example, we will want to set the **Product number** to **0050209O**.

www.dynamicscompanions.com
Dynamics Companions

- 17 -

www.blindsquirrelpublishing.com
© 2019 Blind Squirrel Publishing, LLC , All Rights Reserved

BLIND SQUIRREL
PUBLISHING

DYNAMICS COMPANIONS
BARE BONES CONFIGURATION GUIDE

CONFIGURING PRODUCT INFORMATION MANAGEMENT WITHIN DYNAMICS 365 FOR FINANCE & OPERATIONS
MODULE 2: CONFIGURING PRODUCTS & SERVICES

Creating a new Product

How to do it...

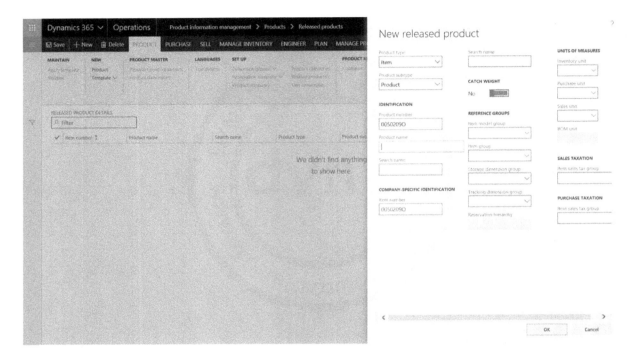

Step 2: Update the Product number

Notice that the company specific **Item number** will default in based off the **Product Number**.

DYNAMICS COMPANIONS
BARE BONES CONFIGURATION GUIDE

CONFIGURING PRODUCT INFORMATION MANAGEMENT WITHIN DYNAMICS 365 FOR FINANCE & OPERATIONS
MODULE 2: CONFIGURING PRODUCTS & SERVICES

Creating a new Product

How to do it...

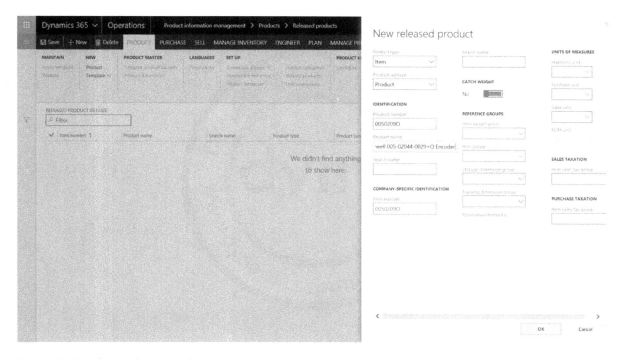

Step 3: Update the Product name

Next we will want to add a more descriptive **Product name** for those of us that don't want to decipher product codes all of the time.

To do this we will just need to update the **Product name** value.

For this example, we will want to set the **Product name** to **Honeywell 005-02044-0029+O Encoder**.

www.dynamicscompanions.com
Dynamics Companions

- 19 -

www.blindsquirrelpublishing.com
© 2019 Blind Squirrel Publishing, LLC , All Rights Reserved

BLIND SQUIRREL
PUBLISHING

DYNAMICS COMPANIONS
BARE BONES CONFIGURATION GUIDE

CONFIGURING PRODUCT INFORMATION MANAGEMENT WITHIN DYNAMICS 365 FOR FINANCE & OPERATIONS
MODULE 2: CONFIGURING PRODUCTS & SERVICES

Creating a new Product

How to do it...

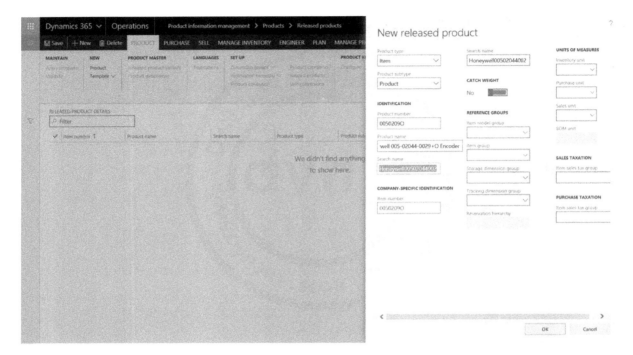

Step 4: Update the Search name

To do this we will want to update the **Search name** value.

For this example, we will want to set the **Search name** to **005-02044-0029+O**.

www.dynamicscompanions.com
Dynamics Companions

- 20 -

www.blindsquirrelpublishing.com
© 2019 Blind Squirrel Publishing, LLC , All Rights Reserved

BLIND SQUIRREL
PUBLISHING

DYNAMICS COMPANIONS
BARE BONES CONFIGURATION GUIDE

CONFIGURING PRODUCT INFORMATION MANAGEMENT WITHIN DYNAMICS 365 FOR FINANCE & OPERATIONS
MODULE 2: CONFIGURING PRODUCTS & SERVICES

Creating a new Product

How to do it...

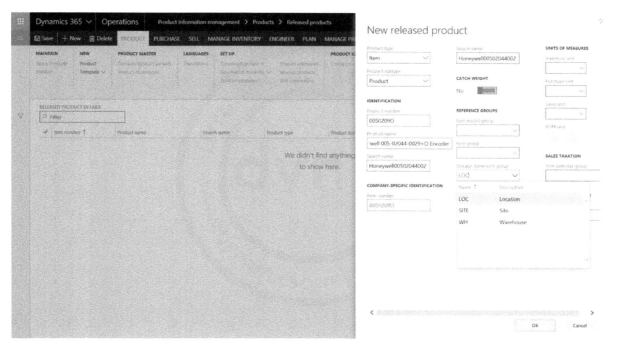

Step 5: Select the Storage dimension group

New we will want to change the **Storage Dimension Group** so that we can track this product within our warehouse locations.

To do this we will just need to select the **Storage dimension group** from the dropdown list.

For this example, we will want to click on the **Storage dimension group** dropdown list and select **LOC**.

www.dynamicscompanions.com
Dynamics Companions

- 21 -

www.blindsquirrelpublishing.com
© 2019 Blind Squirrel Publishing, LLC , All Rights Reserved

BLIND SQUIRREL
PUBLISHING

DYNAMICS COMPANIONS
BARE BONES CONFIGURATION GUIDE

CONFIGURING PRODUCT INFORMATION MANAGEMENT WITHIN DYNAMICS 365 FOR FINANCE & OPERATIONS
MODULE 2: CONFIGURING PRODUCTS & SERVICES

Creating a new Product

How to do it...

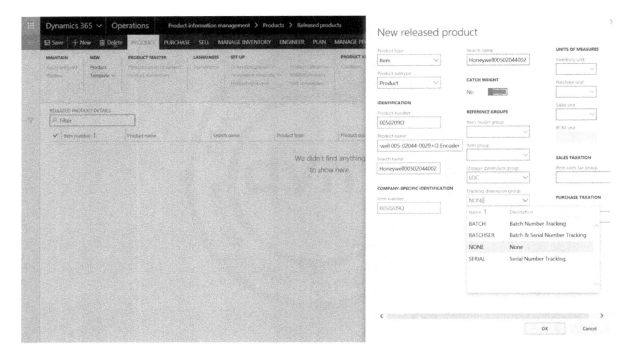

Step 6: Select the Tracking dimension group

Next we will want to select the **Tracking Dimension Group** to no tacking since we will not be using batch or serial number tracking on this item.

To do this we will just need to select the **Tracking dimension group** from the dropdown list.

For this example, we will want to click on the **Tracking dimension group** dropdown list and select **NONE**.

www.dynamicscompanions.com
Dynamics Companions

- 22 -

www.blindsquirrelpublishing.com
© 2019 Blind Squirrel Publishing, LLC , All Rights Reserved

BLIND SQUIRREL
PUBLISHING

DYNAMICS COMPANIONS
BARE BONES CONFIGURATION GUIDE

CONFIGURING PRODUCT INFORMATION MANAGEMENT WITHIN DYNAMICS 365 FOR FINANCE & OPERATIONS
MODULE 2: CONFIGURING PRODUCTS & SERVICES

Creating a new Product

How to do it...

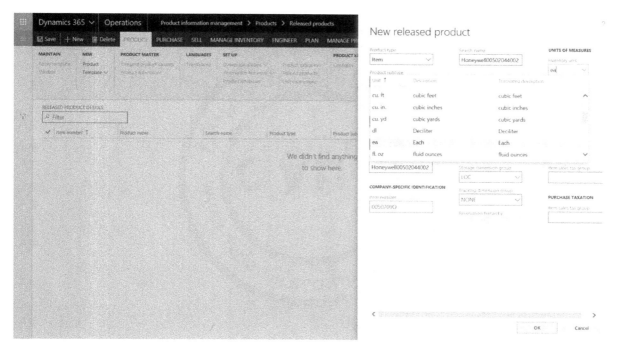

Step 7: Select the Inventory unit

Now we will want to specify the unit of measure that we want to track our inventory quantities in.

To do this we will just need to select the **Inventory unit** from the dropdown list.

For this example, we will want to click on the **Inventory unit** dropdown list and select **ea**.

dyn c

www.dynamicscompanions.com
Dynamics Companions

- 23 -

www.blindsquirrelpublishing.com
© 2019 Blind Squirrel Publishing, LLC , All Rights Reserved

BLIND SQUIRREL
PUBLISHING

DYNAMICS COMPANIONS
BARE BONES CONFIGURATION GUIDE

CONFIGURING PRODUCT INFORMATION MANAGEMENT WITHIN DYNAMICS 365 FOR FINANCE & OPERATIONS
MODULE 2: CONFIGURING PRODUCTS & SERVICES

Creating a new Product

How to do it...

Step 8: Select the Purchase unit

Next we will want to choose the unit of measure that we want to track our purchase quantities in.

To do this we will just need to select the **Purchase unit** from the dropdown list.

For this example, we will want to click on the **Purchase unit** dropdown list and select **ea**.

www.dynamicscompanions.com
Dynamics Companions

- 24 -

www.blindsquirrelpublishing.com
© 2019 Blind Squirrel Publishing, LLC , All Rights Reserved

BLIND SQUIRREL
PUBLISHING

DYNAMICS COMPANIONS
BARE BONES CONFIGURATION GUIDE

CONFIGURING PRODUCT INFORMATION MANAGEMENT WITHIN DYNAMICS 365 FOR FINANCE & OPERATIONS
MODULE 2: CONFIGURING PRODUCTS & SERVICES

Creating a new Product

How to do it...

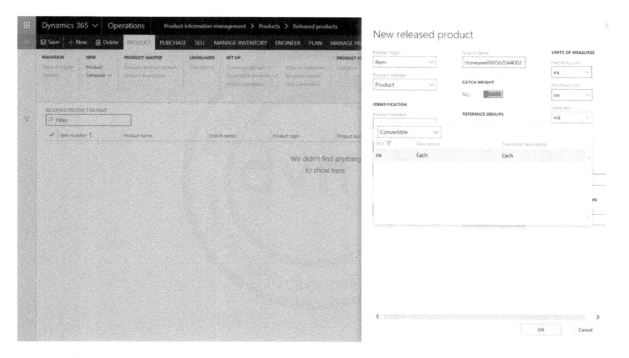

Step 9: Select the Sales unit

Now we will want to select the unit of measure that we want to track our sales quantities in.

To do this we will just need to select the **Sales unit** from the dropdown list.

For this example, we will want to click on the **Sales unit** dropdown list and select **ea**.

www.dynamicscompanions.com
Dynamics Companions

- 25 -

www.blindsquirrelpublishing.com
© 2019 Blind Squirrel Publishing, LLC , All Rights Reserved

BLIND SQUIRREL
PUBLISHING

DYNAMICS COMPANIONS
BARE BONES CONFIGURATION GUIDE

CONFIGURING PRODUCT INFORMATION MANAGEMENT WITHIN DYNAMICS 365 FOR FINANCE & OPERATIONS
MODULE 2: CONFIGURING PRODUCTS & SERVICES

Creating a new Product

How to do it...

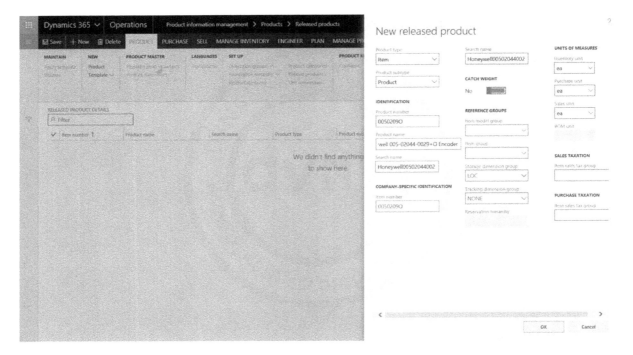

Step 10: Click OK

Now we have specified all of the main configuration fields for the product we can create the record.

To do this just click on the **OK** button.

www.dynamicscompanions.com
Dynamics Companions

- 26 -

www.blindsquirrelpublishing.com
© 2019 Blind Squirrel Publishing, LLC , All Rights Reserved

BLIND SQUIRREL
PUBLISHING

DYNAMICS COMPANIONS
BARE BONES CONFIGURATION GUIDE

CONFIGURING PRODUCT INFORMATION MANAGEMENT WITHIN DYNAMICS 365 FOR FINANCE & OPERATIONS
MODULE 2: CONFIGURING PRODUCTS & SERVICES

Creating a new Product

How to do it...

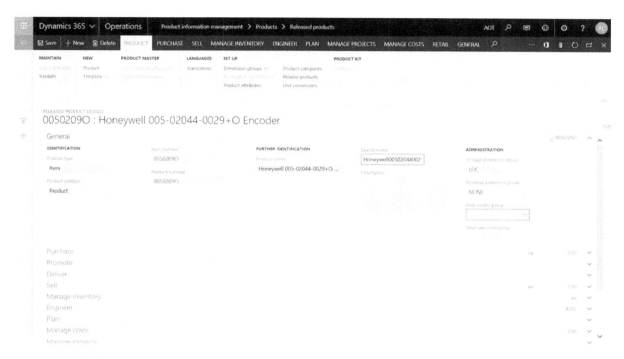

Step 10: Click OK

This will take us to the new **Released product** record maintenance form where we will be able to see all of the details of the product.

www.dynamicscompanions.com
Dynamics Companions

- 27 -

www.blindsquirrelpublishing.com
© 2019 Blind Squirrel Publishing, LLC , All Rights Reserved

BLIND SQUIRREL
PUBLISHING

DYNAMICS COMPANIONS
BARE BONES CONFIGURATION GUIDE

CONFIGURING PRODUCT INFORMATION MANAGEMENT WITHIN DYNAMICS 365 FOR FINANCE & OPERATIONS
MODULE 2: CONFIGURING PRODUCTS & SERVICES

Creating a new Product

Review

How easy was that. We just created a new product that we can now start using within the system.

DYNAMICS COMPANIONS
BARE BONES CONFIGURATION GUIDE

CONFIGURING PRODUCT INFORMATION MANAGEMENT WITHIN DYNAMICS 365 FOR FINANCE & OPERATIONS
MODULE 2: CONFIGURING PRODUCTS & SERVICES

Manually Updating Product Details

After you have created your **Product** you can now update all of the other product information through the maintenance forms.

How to do it...

Step 1: Click on the Item number

Once we have created the **Released product** we can see it within the **Released products** list page.

If we want to edit any of the product details then we can open up the details form just by selecting the item.

Click on the **Item number** link

This will open up the product details form and you will see that there is a lot more information available to you.

One thing that you may want to do is to set the default **Purchase Price** on the product.

Expand out the **Purchase** tab group

Step 2: Update the Price

From here we can update any of the other fields on the **Released products** record.

If we want to update the purchase price for the product then we just do it.

Set the **Price** to **26.61**

Since we updated the **Purchase price** for the product, we may also want to update the **Sales price** as well. We will find all of the **Sales** fields within the **Sell** fast tab.

Expand the **Sell** fast tab

Step 3: Update the Price

From here we can change all of the Sales settings for the product.

Now we can change the default base sales price for the released product.

Set the **Price** to **42.92**

www.dynamicscompanions.com
Dynamics Companions

- 29 -

www.blindsquirrelpublishing.com
© 2019 Blind Squirrel Publishing, LLC , All Rights Reserved

BLIND SQUIRREL
PUBLISHING

DYNAMICS COMPANIONS
BARE BONES CONFIGURATION GUIDE

CONFIGURING PRODUCT INFORMATION MANAGEMENT WITHIN DYNAMICS 365 FOR FINANCE & OPERATIONS
MODULE 2: CONFIGURING PRODUCTS & SERVICES

Manually Updating Product Details

How to do it...

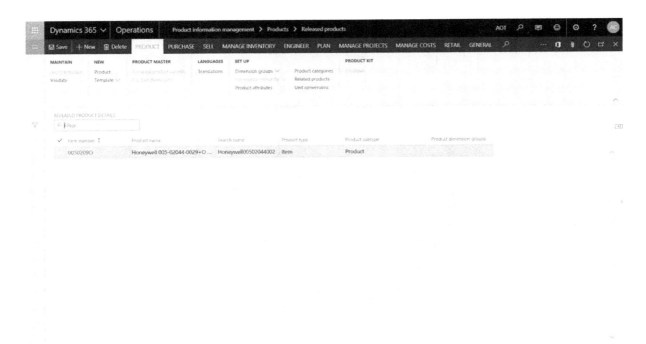

Step 1: Click on the Item number

Once we have created the **Released product** we can see it within the **Released products** list page.

If we want to edit any of the product details then we can open up the details form just by selecting the item.

To do this return to the **Released Products** list page, and double click on the item that you want to edit from the list.

www.dynamicscompanions.com
Dynamics Companions

- 30 -

www.blindsquirrelpublishing.com
© 2019 Blind Squirrel Publishing, LLC , All Rights Reserved

BLIND SQUIRREL
PUBLISHING

DYNAMICS COMPANIONS
BARE BONES CONFIGURATION GUIDE

CONFIGURING PRODUCT INFORMATION MANAGEMENT WITHIN DYNAMICS 365 FOR FINANCE & OPERATIONS
MODULE 2: CONFIGURING PRODUCTS & SERVICES

Manually Updating Product Details

How to do it...

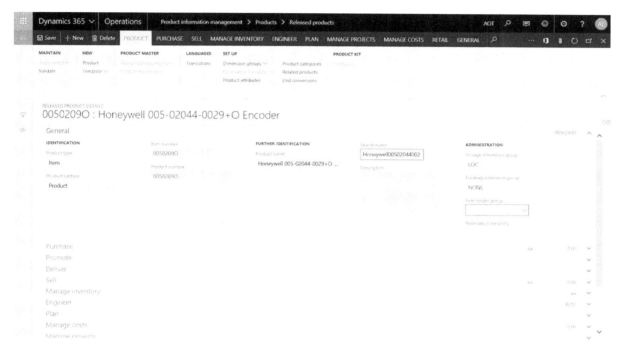

Step 1: Click on the Item number

This will open up the product details form and you will see that there is a lot more information available to you.

www.dynamicscompanions.com
Dynamics Companions

- 31 -

www.blindsquirrelpublishing.com
© 2019 Blind Squirrel Publishing, LLC , All Rights Reserved

BLIND SQUIRREL
PUBLISHING

DYNAMICS COMPANIONS
BARE BONES CONFIGURATION GUIDE

CONFIGURING PRODUCT INFORMATION MANAGEMENT WITHIN DYNAMICS 365 FOR FINANCE & OPERATIONS
MODULE 2: CONFIGURING PRODUCTS & SERVICES

Manually Updating Product Details

How to do it...

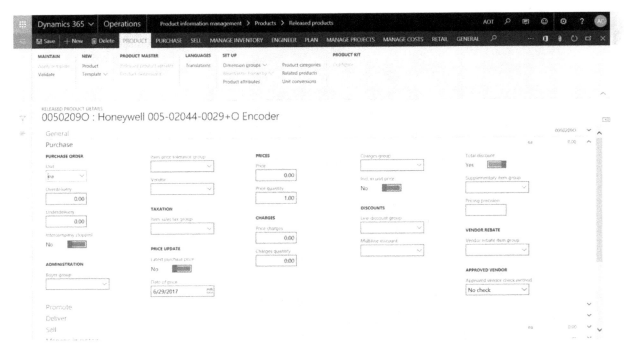

Step 1: Click on the Item number

One thing that you may want to do is to set the default **Purchase Price** on the product.

To do this, expand out the **Purchase** tab group so that you can see all of the purchasing fields.

www.dynamicscompanions.com
Dynamics Companions

- 32 -

www.blindsquirrelpublishing.com
© 2019 Blind Squirrel Publishing, LLC , All Rights Reserved

BLIND SQUIRREL
PUBLISHING

DYNAMICS COMPANIONS
BARE BONES CONFIGURATION GUIDE

CONFIGURING PRODUCT INFORMATION MANAGEMENT WITHIN DYNAMICS 365 FOR FINANCE & OPERATIONS
MODULE 2: CONFIGURING PRODUCTS & SERVICES

Manually Updating Product Details

How to do it...

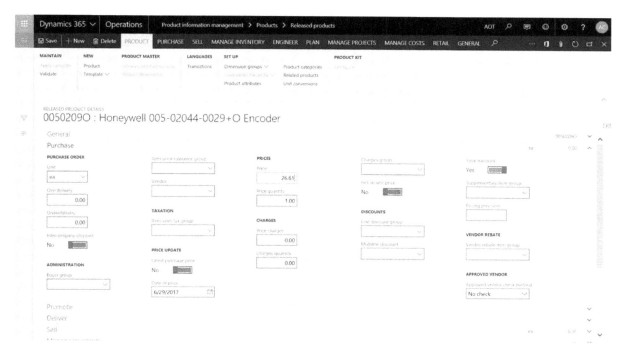

Step 2: Update the Price

From here we can update any of the other fields on the **Released products** record.

If we want to update the purchase price for the product then we just do it.

To do this we will just need to update the **Price** value.

For this example, we will want to set the **Price** to **26.61**.

www.dynamicscompanions.com
Dynamics Companions

- 33 -

www.blindsquirrelpublishing.com
© 2019 Blind Squirrel Publishing, LLC , All Rights Reserved

BLIND SQUIRREL
PUBLISHING

DYNAMICS COMPANIONS
BARE BONES CONFIGURATION GUIDE

CONFIGURING PRODUCT INFORMATION MANAGEMENT WITHIN DYNAMICS 365 FOR FINANCE & OPERATIONS
MODULE 2: CONFIGURING PRODUCTS & SERVICES

Manually Updating Product Details

How to do it...

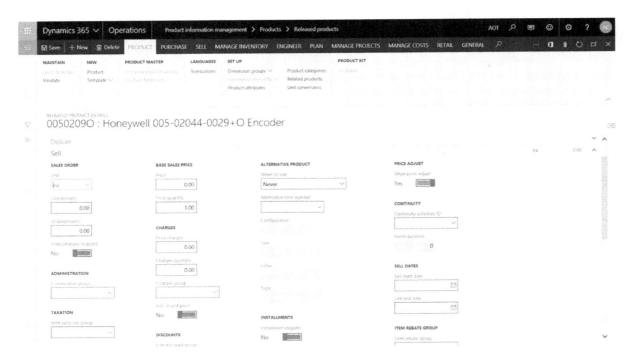

Step 2: Update the Price

Since we updated the **Purchase price** for the product, we may also want to update the **Sales price** as well. We will find all of the **Sales** fields within the **Sell** fast tab.

To see this information, scroll down and expand the **Sell** tab group.

DYNAMICS COMPANIONS
BARE BONES CONFIGURATION GUIDE

CONFIGURING PRODUCT INFORMATION MANAGEMENT WITHIN DYNAMICS 365 FOR FINANCE & OPERATIONS
MODULE 2: CONFIGURING PRODUCTS & SERVICES

Manually Updating Product Details

How to do it...

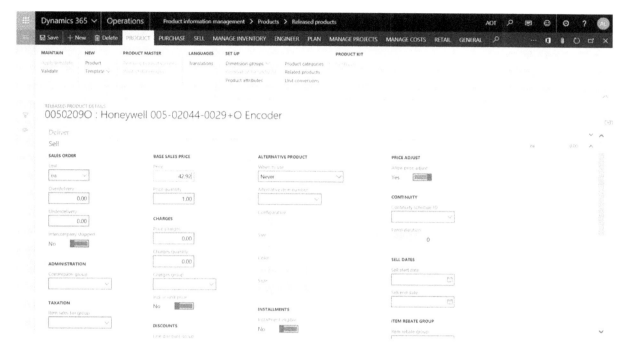

Step 3: Update the Price

From here we can change all of the Sales settings for the product.

Now we can change the default base sales price for the released product.

To do this we will just need to update the **Price** value.

For this example, we will want to set the **Price** to **42.92**.

You can keep on tweaking the data within your product as much as you like.

dyn c

www.dynamicscompanions.com
Dynamics Companions

- 35 -

www.blindsquirrelpublishing.com
© 2019 Blind Squirrel Publishing, LLC , All Rights Reserved

BLIND SQUIRREL
PUBLISHING

DYNAMICS COMPANIONS
BARE BONES CONFIGURATION GUIDE

CONFIGURING PRODUCT INFORMATION MANAGEMENT WITHIN DYNAMICS 365 FOR FINANCE & OPERATIONS
MODULE 2: CONFIGURING PRODUCTS & SERVICES

Manually Updating Product Details

Review

Now you know how to edit the default information on the product records. The fast tabs give us an easy way to group all of the different data relating to the records and also give us an easy way to find the different fields quickly.

DYNAMICS COMPANIONS
BARE BONES CONFIGURATION GUIDE

CONFIGURING PRODUCT INFORMATION MANAGEMENT WITHIN DYNAMICS 365 FOR FINANCE & OPERATIONS
MODULE 2: CONFIGURING PRODUCTS & SERVICES

Adding A Product Image

Something else that you may want to do with your product is add a product image to the record to give users a more visual view of the product.

How to do it...

Step 1: Click Change image

We can change the product image from the **Product image** fast tab.

Click on the **Change image** button within the **Product image** fast tab.

Step 2: Click New

From here we can add as many images to the Released Product record.

Click on the **New** button.

Step 3: Click Browse

Click on the **Browse** button.

Step 4: Open the Image

This will open up a file explorer for you and you can browse for your images.

Find the image and click **Open**

When you return back to the **Product images** form you will be able to see the image will now be showing.

If you have multiple images then you can change the default image that is associated with product.

Check the **Default Image** flag and click **OK**

When you return back to the **Released Product Details** form you will also see that the product image is shown in the General tab group.

How cool is that?

www.dynamicscompanions.com
Dynamics Companions

- 37 -

www.blindsquirrelpublishing.com
© 2019 Blind Squirrel Publishing, LLC , All Rights Reserved

BLIND SQUIRREL
PUBLISHING

DYNAMICS COMPANIONS
BARE BONES CONFIGURATION GUIDE

CONFIGURING PRODUCT INFORMATION MANAGEMENT WITHIN DYNAMICS 365 FOR FINANCE & OPERATIONS
MODULE 2: CONFIGURING PRODUCTS & SERVICES

Adding A Product Image

How to do it...

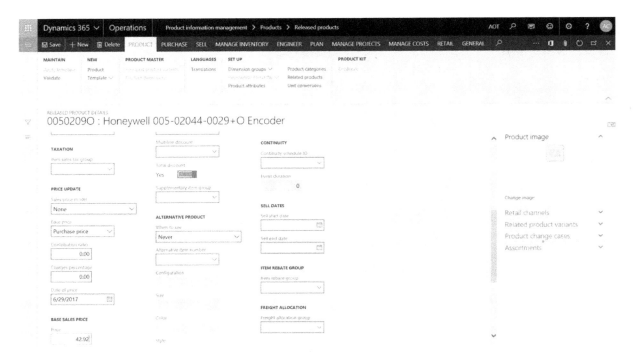

Step 1: Click Change image

We can change the product image from the **Product image** fast tab.

To do this just click on the **Change image** button within the **Product image** fast tab.

dync
www.dynamicscompanions.com
Dynamics Companions

- 38 -

www.blindsquirrelpublishing.com
© 2019 Blind Squirrel Publishing, LLC , All Rights Reserved

BLIND SQUIRREL
PUBLISHING

DYNAMICS COMPANIONS
BARE BONES CONFIGURATION GUIDE

CONFIGURING PRODUCT INFORMATION MANAGEMENT WITHIN DYNAMICS 365 FOR FINANCE & OPERATIONS
MODULE 2: CONFIGURING PRODUCTS & SERVICES

Adding A Product Image

How to do it...

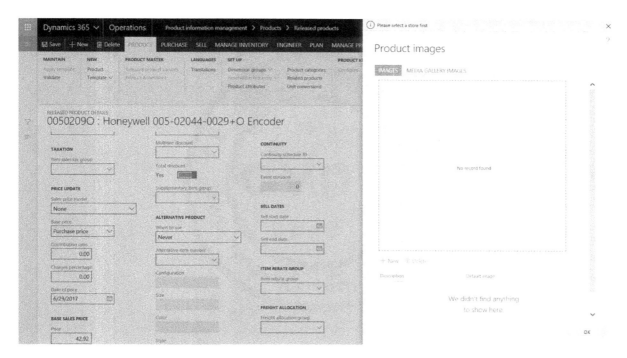

Step 2: Click New

From here we can add as many images to the Released Product record.

To do this just click on the **New** button.

www.dynamicscompanions.com
Dynamics Companions

- 39 -

www.blindsquirrelpublishing.com
© 2019 Blind Squirrel Publishing, LLC , All Rights Reserved

BLIND SQUIRREL
PUBLISHING

DYNAMICS COMPANIONS
BARE BONES CONFIGURATION GUIDE

CONFIGURING PRODUCT INFORMATION MANAGEMENT WITHIN DYNAMICS 365 FOR FINANCE & OPERATIONS
MODULE 2: CONFIGURING PRODUCTS & SERVICES

Adding A Product Image

How to do it...

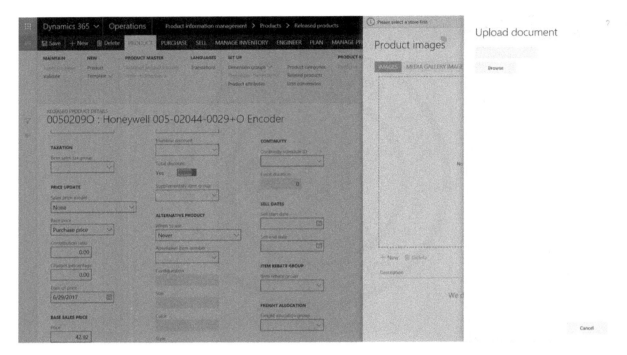

Step 3: Click Browse

To do this just click on the **Browse** button.

dyn

www.dynamicscompanions.com
Dynamics Companions

- 40 -

www.blindsquirrelpublishing.com
© 2019 Blind Squirrel Publishing, LLC , All Rights Reserved

BLIND SQUIRREL
PUBLISHING

DYNAMICS COMPANIONS
BARE BONES CONFIGURATION GUIDE

CONFIGURING PRODUCT INFORMATION MANAGEMENT WITHIN DYNAMICS 365 FOR FINANCE & OPERATIONS
MODULE 2: CONFIGURING PRODUCTS & SERVICES

Adding A Product Image

How to do it...

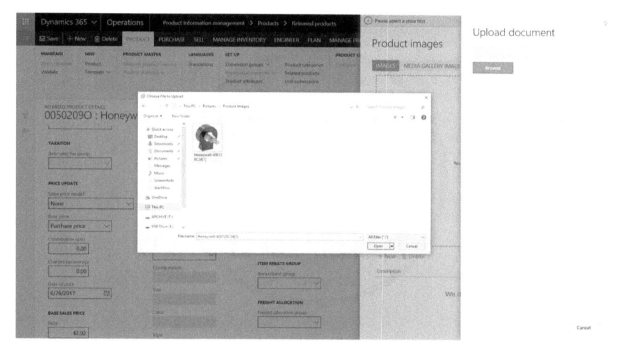

Step 4: Open the Image

This will open up a file explorer for you and you can browse for your images.

All you need to do is find the product image that you want to use and then click on the **Open** button.

www.dynamicscompanions.com
Dynamics Companions

- 41 -

www.blindsquirrelpublishing.com
© 2019 Blind Squirrel Publishing, LLC , All Rights Reserved

BLIND SQUIRREL
PUBLISHING

DYNAMICS COMPANIONS
BARE BONES CONFIGURATION GUIDE

CONFIGURING PRODUCT INFORMATION MANAGEMENT WITHIN DYNAMICS 365 FOR FINANCE & OPERATIONS
MODULE 2: CONFIGURING PRODUCTS & SERVICES

Adding A Product Image

How to do it...

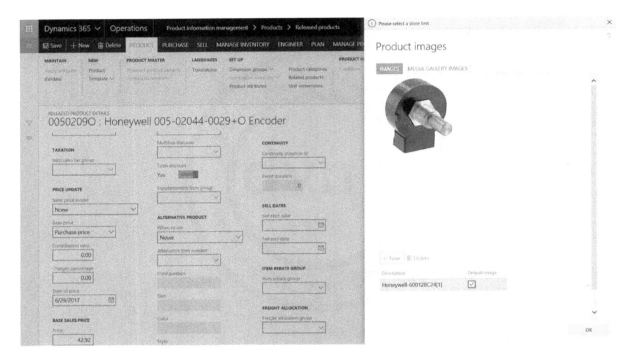

Step 4: Open the Image

When you return back to the **Product images** form you will be able to see the image will now be showing.

If you have multiple images then you can change the default image that is associated with product.

To do this, just check the **Default Image** flag.

After we have done that we can click on the **OK** button to exit from the form.

www.dynamicscompanions.com
Dynamics Companions

- 42 -

www.blindsquirrelpublishing.com
© 2019 Blind Squirrel Publishing, LLC , All Rights Reserved

BLIND SQUIRREL
PUBLISHING

DYNAMICS COMPANIONS
BARE BONES CONFIGURATION GUIDE

CONFIGURING PRODUCT INFORMATION MANAGEMENT WITHIN DYNAMICS 365 FOR FINANCE & OPERATIONS
MODULE 2: CONFIGURING PRODUCTS & SERVICES

Adding A Product Image

How to do it...

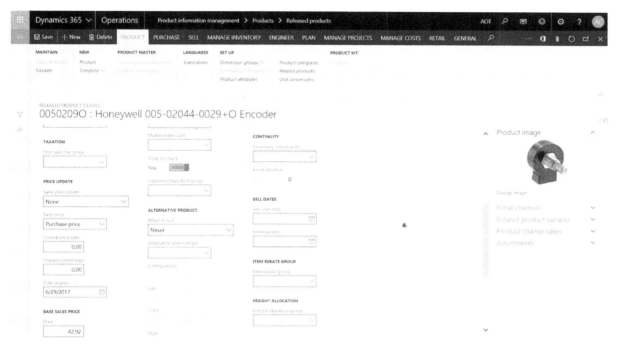

Step 4: Open the Image

When you return back to the **Released Product Details** form you will also see that the product image is shown in the General tab group.

How cool is that?

DYNAMICS COMPANIONS
BARE BONES CONFIGURATION GUIDE

CONFIGURING PRODUCT INFORMATION MANAGEMENT WITHIN DYNAMICS 365 FOR FINANCE & OPERATIONS
MODULE 2: CONFIGURING PRODUCTS & SERVICES

Adding A Product Image

Review

Now you are able to add a little bit of color to your products with the images.

DYNAMICS COMPANIONS
BARE BONES CONFIGURATION GUIDE

CONFIGURING PRODUCT INFORMATION MANAGEMENT WITHIN DYNAMICS 365 FOR FINANCE & OPERATIONS
MODULE 2: CONFIGURING PRODUCTS & SERVICES

Importing Products Using The Data Import Export Framework

Adding products by hand is pretty easy, but if you have a lot of products that you want to load into Dynamics 365, then you may want to use the **Data Import Export Framework** to load them in from a CSV file, or an Excel spreadsheet.

How to do it...

Step 1: Click on Data management

We can get to the **Data management** form a couple of different ways. The easiest way is through the default workspace.

Click on the **Data management** tile

Step 2: Open the Data management form through the menu

The first way is through the master menu.

Navigate to System administration > Data management

Step 3: Open the Data Management form through the menu search

Another way that we can find the **Data Management** form is through the menu search feature.

Type in **data man** into the menu search and select **Data Management**

This will open up the **Data management** workspace where we are able to create import and export projects for Dynamics 365.

Step 4: Click Export

Before we can start importing in our new product records, we will need to have a template that we can use for the import.

A quick and easy way to create a template is to create an export of the existing products and that will show us all of the required fields.

Click on the **Export** tile.

This will open up the **Export** data management form where we can start building our export template.

Step 5: Update the Name

We will want to start off by giving our **Export** project an unique name.

Set the Name to ReleasedProductExport

Step 6: Select the Target data format

Next we will want to select the format of the export that we are going to create.

Click on the **Target data format** dropdown list and select **EXCEL**

DYNAMICS COMPANIONS
BARE BONES CONFIGURATION GUIDE

CONFIGURING PRODUCT INFORMATION MANAGEMENT WITHIN DYNAMICS 365 FOR FINANCE & OPERATIONS
MODULE 2: CONFIGURING PRODUCTS & SERVICES

Step 7: Select the Entity name

Now we will want to select the **Entity** that we want to use to get the data for our export from.

Click on the **Entity name** dropdown list and select **Released product creation**

Step 8: Click Add entity

Now that we have configured all of the information for our export, all that is left is to create the export entity and add it to the export project.

Click on the **Add entity** button.

Step 9: Click Export

This will add the entity to the project. If we want to we can add more entities to the project to make it so that we can import multiple record types at once, but for now we are done.

Now we will want to start creating our export file.

Click on the **Export** button.

Step 10: Click Close

This will start the export project running, and show us a dialog box to remind us, which we can just dismiss.

Click on the **Close** button.

Step 11: Click Refresh

Now we will be taken to the **Execution summary** page where we will be able to see the progress of the export job.

To see the progress of the job, we can just refresh the page.

Click on the **Refresh** icon.

Step 12: Click Download package

After a couple of seconds and a refresh or two we will get a notification that the export has

been completed and we will also see how many products were exported.

Now that we have created the export, we will want to get a copy of the export package so that we can then use it as our import template.

Click on the **Download package** button.

Step 13: Click Yes

This will then show us a dialog box that says that we haven't created the download package yet, and if we really want to create it.

We definitely do.

Click on the **Yes** button.

This will create an export package for us.

We will want to save this file locally.

Click on the **Save** button and select **Save as.**

This will open up a file explorer for us allowing us to save the file.

Step 14: Update the File name

Now we will want to give our export file a less cryptic name and save it to our desktop.

Set the File name to ReleasedProcustCreation

If we look at the files on our desktop, we will see that there is a **Zip** file that contains all of the information from our export project.

All we need to do here is unzip the contents.

Right-mouse-click on the file and select the **Extract** option.

Step 15: Click Extract

When the extract dialog box is displayed, just select the default location and extract the files.

Click on the **Extract** button.

After the files have been extracted, the folder should open up automatically and we will see

DYNAMICS COMPANIONS
BARE BONES CONFIGURATION GUIDE

CONFIGURING PRODUCT INFORMATION MANAGEMENT WITHIN DYNAMICS 365 FOR FINANCE & OPERATIONS
MODULE 2: CONFIGURING PRODUCTS & SERVICES

that there are a number of files in the extracted zip file.

The one that we are interested in is the **Excel** file and we will want to open it up.

Double click on the excel file.

Step 16: Click Enable Editing

When the Excel file opens up we will see that all of the fields are already populated and we can also see the data from our product that we just added giving us an idea of the required fields.

All we need to do is switch to edit mode.

Click on the **Enable Editing** button.

Now we will be able to make changes to the file.

Now we just want to add all of the new products that we want to import into the template.

Add the sample data and save the file.

Now that we have updated the template data and added our own data into the template we will want to repackage up the files.

Zip up the package files.

Step 17: Click Import

Now that we have a new package with our new data to import, we will want to create an **Import** project.

Click on the **Import** tile.

This will take us to the **Import** project page.

Step 18: Update the Name

The first thing that we will want to do is to give our project a job name.

Set the Name to ReleasedProductImport

Step 19: Select the Source data format

Now we will want to select the type of source data that we will be importing.

Click on the **Source data format** dropdown list and select **Package**

Step 20: Click Upload

Now we will want to add our data package to the project.

Click on the **Upload** button.

This will open up the file explorer and we should be able to see the data packages.

All we need to do here is select the data package that we want to use.

Select the import package and then click on the **Open** button.

Step 21: Click Import

This will start a process where the data management looks at the file and makes sure that it is in the right format, and within a couple of seconds, the package will show up in the selected entities.

Now all that is left is to start the import process.

Click on the **Import** button.

Step 22: Click Close

This will open up a dialog box telling us that the import job is being submitted to the queue.

We can dismiss this dialog.

Click on the **Close** button.

Step 23: Click Refresh

Then we will be taken to the **Execution summary** form where we can see the progress of the import.

www.dynamicscompanions.com
Dynamics Companions

- 47 -

www.blindsquirrelpublishing.com
© 2019 Blind Squirrel Publishing, LLC , All Rights Reserved

BLIND SQUIRREL
PUBLISHING

DYNAMICS COMPANIONS
BARE BONES CONFIGURATION GUIDE

CONFIGURING PRODUCT INFORMATION MANAGEMENT WITHIN DYNAMICS 365 FOR FINANCE & OPERATIONS
MODULE 2: CONFIGURING PRODUCTS & SERVICES

All we need to do is wait for the import to process and maybe refresh the form.

Click on the **Refresh** icon.

After a little bit, we will see that all of the products have been moved into the staging tables.

And then a little while later we will also see that all of the products have been moved into the **Released products** table.

Step 24: Open the Released products form through the menu

If you don't believe it, then just open up the **Released products** form.

Navigate to Product information management > Products > Released products

www.dynamicscompanions.com
Dynamics Companions

- 48 -

www.blindsquirrelpublishing.com
© 2019 Blind Squirrel Publishing, LLC , All Rights Reserved

BLIND SQUIRREL
PUBLISHING

DYNAMICS COMPANIONS
BARE BONES CONFIGURATION GUIDE

CONFIGURING PRODUCT INFORMATION MANAGEMENT WITHIN DYNAMICS 365 FOR FINANCE & OPERATIONS
MODULE 2: CONFIGURING PRODUCTS & SERVICES

Importing Products Using The Data Import Export Framework

How to do it...

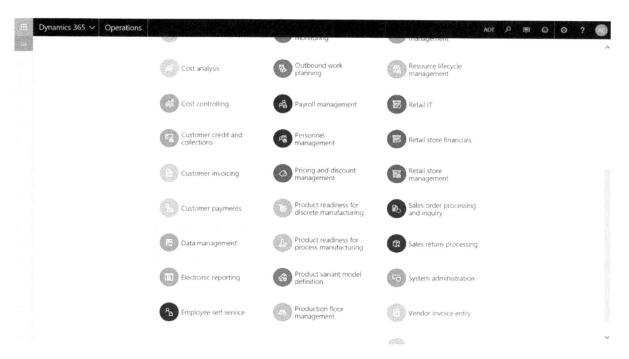

Step 1: Click on Data management

We can get to the **Data management** form a couple of different ways. The easiest way is through the default workspace.

To do this, just open up the default workspace and then click on the **Data management** tile.

www.dynamicscompanions.com
Dynamics Companions

- 49 -

www.blindsquirrelpublishing.com
© 2019 Blind Squirrel Publishing, LLC , All Rights Reserved

BLIND SQUIRREL
PUBLISHING

DYNAMICS COMPANIONS
BARE BONES CONFIGURATION GUIDE

CONFIGURING PRODUCT INFORMATION MANAGEMENT WITHIN DYNAMICS 365 FOR FINANCE & OPERATIONS
MODULE 2: CONFIGURING PRODUCTS & SERVICES

Importing Products Using The Data Import Export Framework

How to do it...

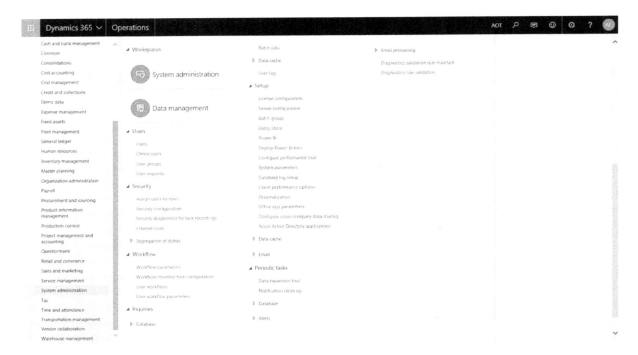

Step 2: Open the Data management form through the menu

The first way is through the master menu.

To do this, open up the navigation panel, expand out the **Modules** and group, and click on **System administration** to see all of the menu items that are available. Then click on the **Data management** menu item.

www.dynamicscompanions.com
Dynamics Companions

- 50 -

www.blindsquirrelpublishing.com
© 2019 Blind Squirrel Publishing, LLC , All Rights Reserved

BLIND SQUIRREL
PUBLISHING

DYNAMICS COMPANIONS
BARE BONES CONFIGURATION GUIDE

CONFIGURING PRODUCT INFORMATION MANAGEMENT WITHIN DYNAMICS 365 FOR FINANCE & OPERATIONS
MODULE 2: CONFIGURING PRODUCTS & SERVICES

Importing Products Using The Data Import Export Framework

How to do it...

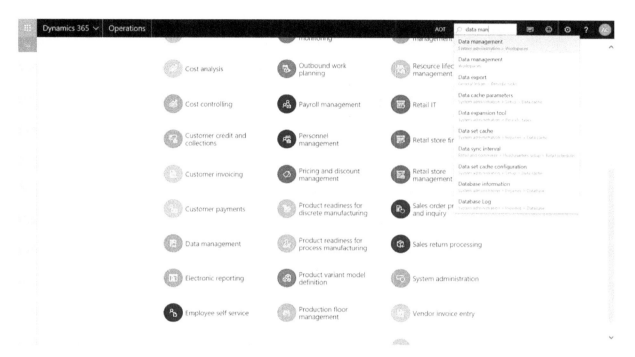

Step 3: Open the Data Management form through the menu search

Another way that we can find the **Data Management** form is through the menu search feature.

We can do this by clicking on the search icon in the header of the form (or by pressing **ALT+G**) and then type in **data man** storage into the search box. Then you will be able to select the **Data Management** form from the dropdown list.

www.dynamicscompanions.com
Dynamics Companions

- 51 -

www.blindsquirrelpublishing.com
© 2019 Blind Squirrel Publishing, LLC , All Rights Reserved

BLIND SQUIRREL
PUBLISHING

DYNAMICS COMPANIONS
BARE BONES CONFIGURATION GUIDE

CONFIGURING PRODUCT INFORMATION MANAGEMENT WITHIN DYNAMICS 365 FOR FINANCE & OPERATIONS
MODULE 2: CONFIGURING PRODUCTS & SERVICES

Importing Products Using The Data Import Export Framework

How to do it...

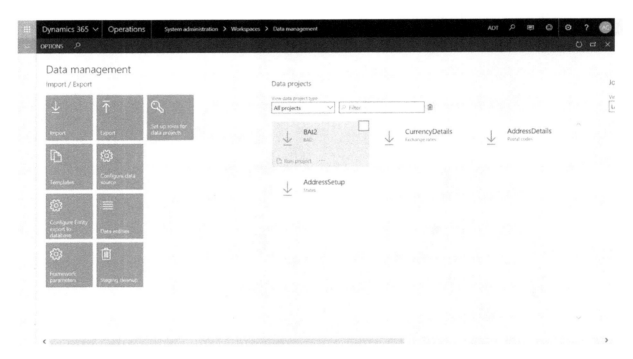

Step 3: Open the Data Management form through the menu search

This will open up the **Data management** workspace where we are able to create import and export projects for Dynamics 365.

www.dynamicscompanions.com
Dynamics Companions

- 52 -

www.blindsquirrelpublishing.com
© 2019 Blind Squirrel Publishing, LLC , All Rights Reserved

BLIND SQUIRREL
PUBLISHING

DYNAMICS COMPANIONS
BARE BONES CONFIGURATION GUIDE

CONFIGURING PRODUCT INFORMATION MANAGEMENT WITHIN DYNAMICS 365 FOR FINANCE & OPERATIONS
MODULE 2: CONFIGURING PRODUCTS & SERVICES

Importing Products Using The Data Import Export Framework

How to do it...

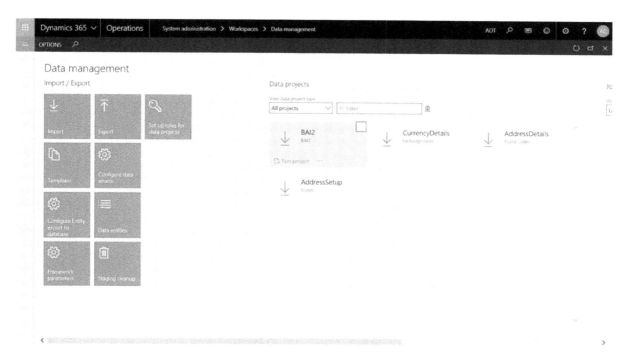

Step 4: Click Export

Before we can start importing in our new product records, we will need to have a template that we can use for the import.

A quick and easy way to create a template is to create an export of the existing products and that will show us all of the required fields.

To do this just click on the **Export** tile within the workspace.

www.dynamicscompanions.com
Dynamics Companions

- 53 -

www.blindsquirrelpublishing.com
© 2019 Blind Squirrel Publishing, LLC , All Rights Reserved

BLIND SQUIRREL
PUBLISHING

DYNAMICS COMPANIONS
BARE BONES CONFIGURATION GUIDE

CONFIGURING PRODUCT INFORMATION MANAGEMENT WITHIN DYNAMICS 365 FOR FINANCE & OPERATIONS
MODULE 2: CONFIGURING PRODUCTS & SERVICES

Importing Products Using The Data Import Export Framework

How to do it...

Step 4: Click Export

This will open up the **Export** data management form where we can start building our export template.

www.dynamicscompanions.com
Dynamics Companions

- 54 -

www.blindsquirrelpublishing.com
© 2019 Blind Squirrel Publishing, LLC , All Rights Reserved

BLIND SQUIRREL
PUBLISHING

DYNAMICS COMPANIONS
BARE BONES CONFIGURATION GUIDE

CONFIGURING PRODUCT INFORMATION MANAGEMENT WITHIN DYNAMICS 365 FOR FINANCE & OPERATIONS
MODULE 2: CONFIGURING PRODUCTS & SERVICES

Importing Products Using The Data Import Export Framework

How to do it...

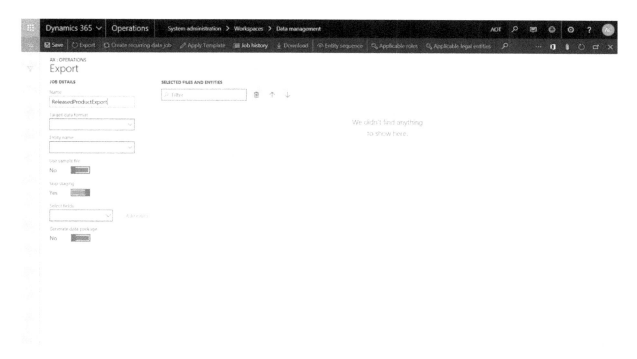

Step 5: Update the Name

We will want to start off by giving our **Export** project an unique name.

To do this we will just need to update the **Name** value.

For this example, we will want to set the **Name** to **ReleasedProductExport**.

dyn c
www.dynamicscompanions.com
Dynamics Companions

- 55 -

www.blindsquirrelpublishing.com
© 2019 Blind Squirrel Publishing, LLC , All Rights Reserved

BLIND SQUIRREL
PUBLISHING

DYNAMICS COMPANIONS
BARE BONES CONFIGURATION GUIDE

CONFIGURING PRODUCT INFORMATION MANAGEMENT WITHIN DYNAMICS 365 FOR FINANCE & OPERATIONS
MODULE 2: CONFIGURING PRODUCTS & SERVICES

Importing Products Using The Data Import Export Framework

How to do it...

Step 6: Select the Target data format

Next we will want to select the format of the export that we are going to create.

We can create the exports in a number of different formats including as a CSV, Excel, and also XML.

To do this we will just need to select the **Target data format** from the dropdown list.

For this example, we will want to export the records as an Excel file which is easier to cut and paste into so we will click on the **Target data format** dropdown list and select the **EXCEL** option.

www.dynamicscompanions.com
Dynamics Companions

- 56 -

www.blindsquirrelpublishing.com
© 2019 Blind Squirrel Publishing, LLC , All Rights Reserved

BLIND SQUIRREL
PUBLISHING

DYNAMICS COMPANIONS
BARE BONES CONFIGURATION GUIDE

CONFIGURING PRODUCT INFORMATION MANAGEMENT WITHIN DYNAMICS 365 FOR FINANCE & OPERATIONS
MODULE 2: CONFIGURING PRODUCTS & SERVICES

Importing Products Using The Data Import Export Framework

How to do it...

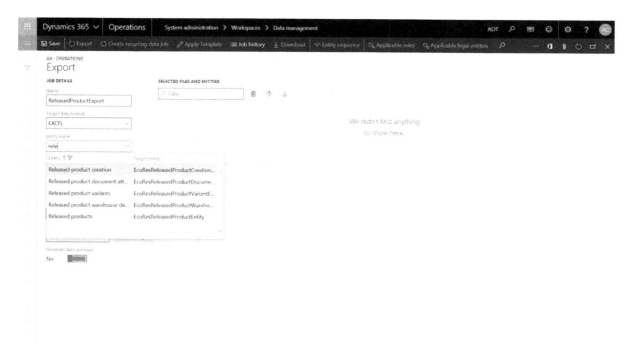

Step 7: Select the Entity name

Now we will want to select the **Entity** that we want to use to get the data for our export from.

To do this we will just need to select the **Entity name** from the dropdown list.

For this example, we will want to click on the **Entity name** dropdown list and select **Released product creation** which will allow us to get all of the released products out of the system, and also allow us to create new products later on.

dync   www.dynamicscompanions.com
Dynamics Companions

- 57 -

www.blindsquirrelpublishing.com
© 2019 Blind Squirrel Publishing, LLC , All Rights Reserved

BLIND SQUIRREL
PUBLISHING

DYNAMICS COMPANIONS
BARE BONES CONFIGURATION GUIDE

CONFIGURING PRODUCT INFORMATION MANAGEMENT WITHIN DYNAMICS 365 FOR FINANCE & OPERATIONS
MODULE 2: CONFIGURING PRODUCTS & SERVICES

Importing Products Using The Data Import Export Framework

How to do it...

Step 8: Click Add entity

Now that we have configured all of the information for our export, all that is left is to create the export entity and add it to the export project.

To do this just click on the **Add entity** button.

www.dynamicscompanions.com
Dynamics Companions

- 58 -

www.blindsquirrelpublishing.com
© 2019 Blind Squirrel Publishing, LLC , All Rights Reserved

BLIND SQUIRREL
PUBLISHING

DYNAMICS COMPANIONS
BARE BONES CONFIGURATION GUIDE

CONFIGURING PRODUCT INFORMATION MANAGEMENT WITHIN DYNAMICS 365 FOR FINANCE & OPERATIONS
MODULE 2: CONFIGURING PRODUCTS & SERVICES

Importing Products Using The Data Import Export Framework

How to do it...

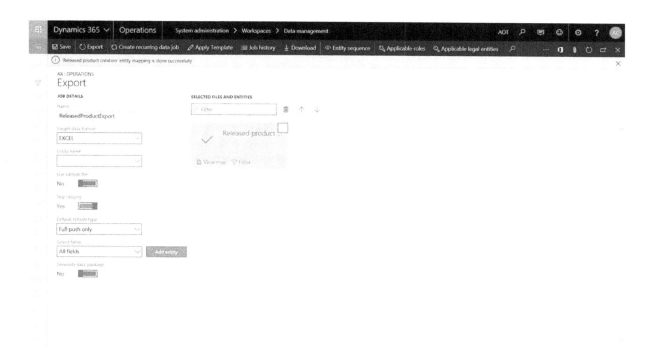

Step 9: Click Export

This will add the entity to the project. If we want to we can add more entities to the project to make it so that we can import multiple record types at once, but for now we are done.

Now we will want to start creating our export file.

To do this just click on the **Export** button in the menu bar.

www.dynamicscompanions.com
Dynamics Companions

- 59 -

www.blindsquirrelpublishing.com
© 2019 Blind Squirrel Publishing, LLC , All Rights Reserved

BLIND SQUIRREL
PUBLISHING

DYNAMICS COMPANIONS
BARE BONES CONFIGURATION GUIDE

CONFIGURING PRODUCT INFORMATION MANAGEMENT WITHIN DYNAMICS 365 FOR FINANCE & OPERATIONS
MODULE 2: CONFIGURING PRODUCTS & SERVICES

Importing Products Using The Data Import Export Framework

How to do it...

Step 10: Click Close

This will start the export project running, and show us a dialog box to remind us, which we can just dismiss.

To do this just click on the **Close** button.

www.dynamicscompanions.com
Dynamics Companions

- 60 -

www.blindsquirrelpublishing.com
© 2019 Blind Squirrel Publishing, LLC , All Rights Reserved

BLIND SQUIRREL
PUBLISHING

DYNAMICS COMPANIONS
BARE BONES CONFIGURATION GUIDE

CONFIGURING PRODUCT INFORMATION MANAGEMENT WITHIN DYNAMICS 365 FOR FINANCE & OPERATIONS
MODULE 2: CONFIGURING PRODUCTS & SERVICES

Importing Products Using The Data Import Export Framework

How to do it...

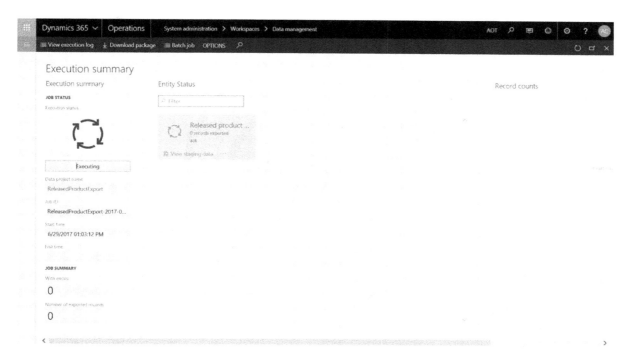

Step 11: Click Refresh

Now we will be taken to the **Execution summary** page where we will be able to see the progress of the export job.

To see the progress of the job, we can just refresh the page.

To do this just click on the **Refresh** icon in the top right of the page.

www.dynamicscompanions.com
Dynamics Companions

- 61 -

www.blindsquirrelpublishing.com
© 2019 Blind Squirrel Publishing, LLC , All Rights Reserved

BLIND SQUIRREL
PUBLISHING

DYNAMICS COMPANIONS
BARE BONES CONFIGURATION GUIDE

CONFIGURING PRODUCT INFORMATION MANAGEMENT WITHIN DYNAMICS 365 FOR FINANCE & OPERATIONS
MODULE 2: CONFIGURING PRODUCTS & SERVICES

Importing Products Using The Data Import Export Framework

How to do it...

Step 12: Click Download package

After a couple of seconds and a refresh or two we will get a notification that the export has been completed and we will also see how many products were exported.

Now that we have created the export, we will want to get a copy of the export package so that we can then use it as our import template.

To do this just click on the **Download package** button in the menu bar.

www.dynamicscompanions.com
Dynamics Companions

- 62 -

www.blindsquirrelpublishing.com
© 2019 Blind Squirrel Publishing, LLC , All Rights Reserved

BLIND SQUIRREL
PUBLISHING

DYNAMICS COMPANIONS
BARE BONES CONFIGURATION GUIDE

CONFIGURING PRODUCT INFORMATION MANAGEMENT WITHIN DYNAMICS 365 FOR FINANCE & OPERATIONS
MODULE 2: CONFIGURING PRODUCTS & SERVICES

Importing Products Using The Data Import Export Framework

How to do it...

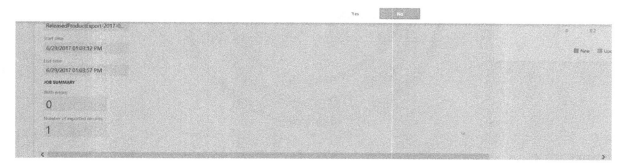

Step 13: Click Yes

This will then show us a dialog box that says that we haven't created the download package yet, and if we really want to create it.

We definitely do.

To do this just click on the **Yes** button.

www.dynamicscompanions.com
Dynamics Companions

- 63 -

www.blindsquirrelpublishing.com
© 2019 Blind Squirrel Publishing, LLC , All Rights Reserved

BLIND SQUIRREL
PUBLISHING

DYNAMICS COMPANIONS
BARE BONES CONFIGURATION GUIDE

CONFIGURING PRODUCT INFORMATION MANAGEMENT WITHIN DYNAMICS 365 FOR FINANCE & OPERATIONS
MODULE 2: CONFIGURING PRODUCTS & SERVICES

Importing Products Using The Data Import Export Framework

How to do it...

Step 13: Click Yes

This will create an export package for us.

dyn c
www.dynamicscompanions.com
Dynamics Companions

- 64 -

www.blindsquirrelpublishing.com
© 2019 Blind Squirrel Publishing, LLC , All Rights Reserved

BLIND SQUIRREL
PUBLISHING

DYNAMICS COMPANIONS
BARE BONES CONFIGURATION GUIDE

CONFIGURING PRODUCT INFORMATION MANAGEMENT WITHIN DYNAMICS 365 FOR FINANCE & OPERATIONS
MODULE 2: CONFIGURING PRODUCTS & SERVICES

Importing Products Using The Data Import Export Framework

How to do it...

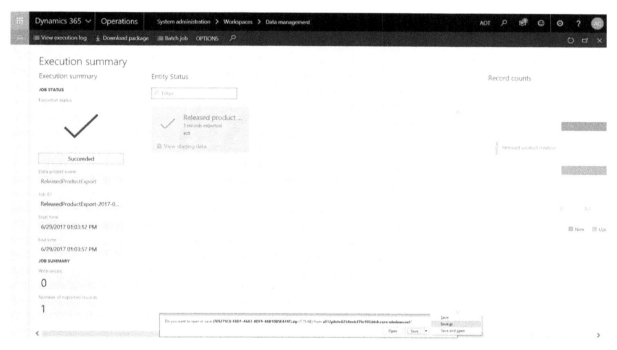

Step 13: Click Yes

We will want to save this file locally.

To do this, just click on the **Save** dropdown box on the file download notification and then select the **Save as** option.

dyn c
www.dynamicscompanions.com
Dynamics Companions

- 65 -

www.blindsquirrelpublishing.com
© 2019 Blind Squirrel Publishing, LLC, All Rights Reserved

BLIND SQUIRREL
PUBLISHING

DYNAMICS COMPANIONS
BARE BONES CONFIGURATION GUIDE

CONFIGURING PRODUCT INFORMATION MANAGEMENT WITHIN DYNAMICS 365 FOR FINANCE & OPERATIONS
MODULE 2: CONFIGURING PRODUCTS & SERVICES

Importing Products Using The Data Import Export Framework

How to do it...

Step 13: Click Yes

This will open up a file explorer for us allowing us to save the file.

dync

www.dynamicscompanions.com
Dynamics Companions

- 66 -

www.blindsquirrelpublishing.com
© 2019 Blind Squirrel Publishing, LLC , All Rights Reserved

BLIND SQUIRREL
PUBLISHING

DYNAMICS COMPANIONS
BARE BONES CONFIGURATION GUIDE

CONFIGURING PRODUCT INFORMATION MANAGEMENT WITHIN DYNAMICS 365 FOR FINANCE & OPERATIONS
MODULE 2: CONFIGURING PRODUCTS & SERVICES

Importing Products Using The Data Import Export Framework

How to do it...

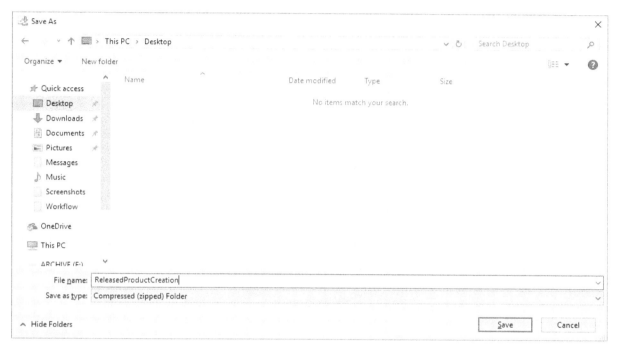

Step 14: Update the File name

Now we will want to give our export file a less cryptic name and save it to our desktop.

To do this we will just need to update the **File name** value and then click on the **Save** button.

For this example, we will want to set the **File name** to **ReleasedProcustCreation.**

dyn c

www.dynamicscompanions.com
Dynamics Companions

- 67 -

www.blindsquirrelpublishing.com
© 2019 Blind Squirrel Publishing, LLC , All Rights Reserved

BLIND SQUIRREL
PUBLISHING

DYNAMICS COMPANIONS
BARE BONES CONFIGURATION GUIDE

CONFIGURING PRODUCT INFORMATION MANAGEMENT WITHIN DYNAMICS 365 FOR FINANCE & OPERATIONS
MODULE 2: CONFIGURING PRODUCTS & SERVICES

Importing Products Using The Data Import Export Framework

How to do it...

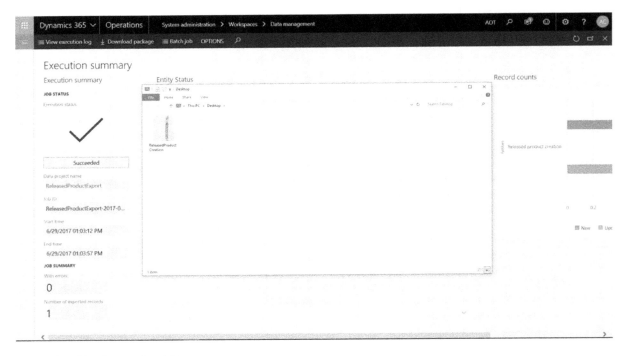

Step 14: Update the File name

If we look at the files on our desktop, we will see that there is a **Zip** file that contains all of the information from our export project.

All we need to do here is unzip the contents.

To do this, just right-mouse-click on the file and select the **Extract** option.

dyn c
www.dynamicscompanions.com
Dynamics Companions

- 68 -

www.blindsquirrelpublishing.com
© 2019 Blind Squirrel Publishing, LLC , All Rights Reserved

BLIND SQUIRREL
PUBLISHING

DYNAMICS COMPANIONS
BARE BONES CONFIGURATION GUIDE

CONFIGURING PRODUCT INFORMATION MANAGEMENT WITHIN DYNAMICS 365 FOR FINANCE & OPERATIONS
MODULE 2: CONFIGURING PRODUCTS & SERVICES

Importing Products Using The Data Import Export Framework

How to do it...

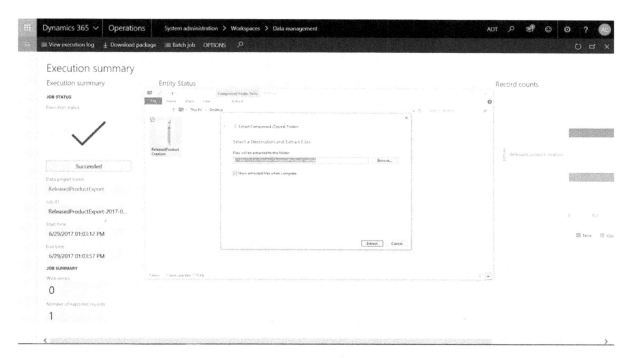

Step 15: Click Extract

When the extract dialog box is displayed, just select the default location and extract the files.

To do this just click on the **Extract** button.

www.dynamicscompanions.com
Dynamics Companions

- 69 -

www.blindsquirrelpublishing.com
© 2019 Blind Squirrel Publishing, LLC , All Rights Reserved

BLIND SQUIRREL
PUBLISHING

DYNAMICS COMPANIONS
BARE BONES CONFIGURATION GUIDE

CONFIGURING PRODUCT INFORMATION MANAGEMENT WITHIN DYNAMICS 365 FOR FINANCE & OPERATIONS
MODULE 2: CONFIGURING PRODUCTS & SERVICES

Importing Products Using The Data Import Export Framework

How to do it...

Step 15: Click Extract

After the files have been extracted, the folder should open up automatically and we will see that there are a number of files in the extracted zip file.

The one that we are interested in is the **Excel** file and we will want to open it up.

To do this, just double click on the excel file.

www.dynamicscompanions.com
Dynamics Companions

- 70 -

www.blindsquirrelpublishing.com
© 2019 Blind Squirrel Publishing, LLC , All Rights Reserved

BLIND SQUIRREL
PUBLISHING

DYNAMICS COMPANIONS
BARE BONES CONFIGURATION GUIDE

CONFIGURING PRODUCT INFORMATION MANAGEMENT WITHIN DYNAMICS 365 FOR FINANCE & OPERATIONS
MODULE 2: CONFIGURING PRODUCTS & SERVICES

Importing Products Using The Data Import Export Framework

How to do it...

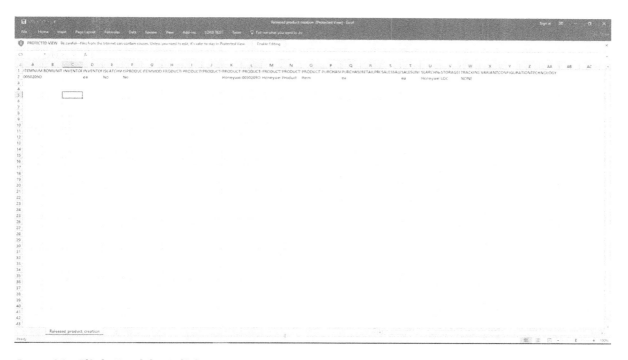

Step 16: Click Enable Editing

When the Excel file opens up we will see that all of the fields are already populated and we can also see the data from our product that we just added giving us an idea of the required fields.

All we need to do is switch to edit mode.

To do this just click on the **Enable Editing** button.

www.dynamicscompanions.com
Dynamics Companions

- 71 -

www.blindsquirrelpublishing.com
© 2019 Blind Squirrel Publishing, LLC , All Rights Reserved

BLIND SQUIRREL
PUBLISHING

DYNAMICS COMPANIONS
BARE BONES CONFIGURATION GUIDE

CONFIGURING PRODUCT INFORMATION MANAGEMENT WITHIN DYNAMICS 365 FOR FINANCE & OPERATIONS
MODULE 2: CONFIGURING PRODUCTS & SERVICES

Importing Products Using The Data Import Export Framework

How to do it...

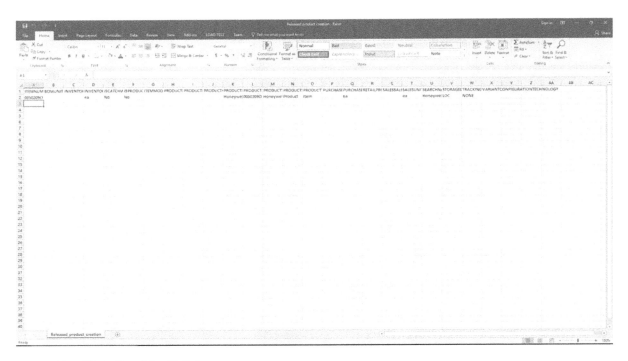

Step 16: Click Enable Editing

Now we will be able to make changes to the file.

www.dynamicscompanions.com
Dynamics Companions

- 72 -

www.blindsquirrelpublishing.com
© 2019 Blind Squirrel Publishing, LLC , All Rights Reserved

BLIND SQUIRREL
PUBLISHING

DYNAMICS COMPANIONS
BARE BONES CONFIGURATION GUIDE

CONFIGURING PRODUCT INFORMATION MANAGEMENT WITHIN DYNAMICS 365 FOR FINANCE & OPERATIONS
MODULE 2: CONFIGURING PRODUCTS & SERVICES

Importing Products Using The Data Import Export Framework

How to do it...

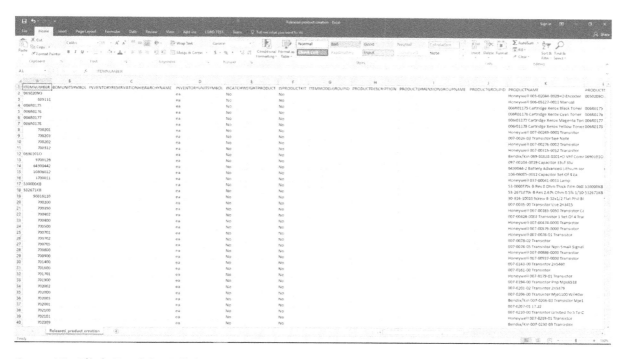

Step 16: Click Enable Editing

Now we just want to add all of the new products that we want to import into the template.

To do this just add the new data into the Excel file and then save the file.

www.dynamicscompanions.com
Dynamics Companions

- 73 -

www.blindsquirrelpublishing.com
© 2019 Blind Squirrel Publishing, LLC , All Rights Reserved

BLIND SQUIRREL
PUBLISHING

DYNAMICS COMPANIONS
BARE BONES CONFIGURATION GUIDE

CONFIGURING PRODUCT INFORMATION MANAGEMENT WITHIN DYNAMICS 365 FOR FINANCE & OPERATIONS
MODULE 2: CONFIGURING PRODUCTS & SERVICES

Importing Products Using The Data Import Export Framework

How to do it...

Step 16: Click Enable Editing

Now that we have updated the template data and added our own data into the template we will want to repackage up the files.

To do this, we will want to select the three files that were in the extracted folder and then zip them up again.

www.dynamicscompanions.com
Dynamics Companions

- 74 -

www.blindsquirrelpublishing.com
© 2019 Blind Squirrel Publishing, LLC , All Rights Reserved

BLIND SQUIRREL
PUBLISHING

DYNAMICS COMPANIONS
BARE BONES CONFIGURATION GUIDE

CONFIGURING PRODUCT INFORMATION MANAGEMENT WITHIN DYNAMICS 365 FOR FINANCE & OPERATIONS
MODULE 2: CONFIGURING PRODUCTS & SERVICES

Importing Products Using The Data Import Export Framework

How to do it...

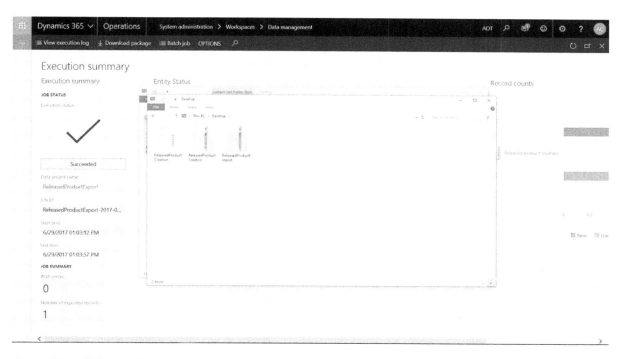

Step 16: Click Enable Editing

Then we will want to move the zip file up to our desktop again.

www.dynamicscompanions.com
Dynamics Companions

www.blindsquirrelpublishing.com
© 2019 Blind Squirrel Publishing, LLC , All Rights Reserved

BLIND SQUIRREL
PUBLISHING

DYNAMICS COMPANIONS
BARE BONES CONFIGURATION GUIDE

CONFIGURING PRODUCT INFORMATION MANAGEMENT WITHIN DYNAMICS 365 FOR FINANCE & OPERATIONS
MODULE 2: CONFIGURING PRODUCTS & SERVICES

Importing Products Using The Data Import Export Framework

How to do it...

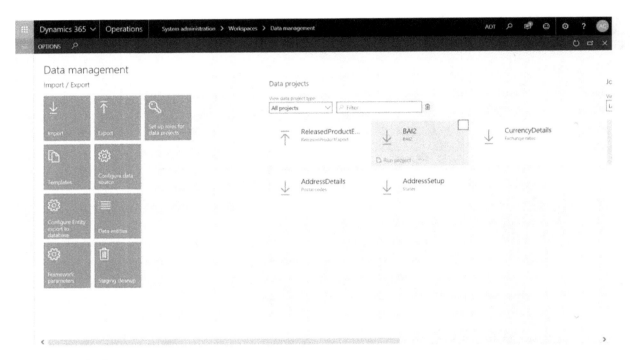

Step 17: Click Import

Now that we have a new package with our new data to import, we will want to create an **Import** project.

To do this just return to the **Data** management workspace and click on the **Import** tile.

www.dynamicscompanions.com
Dynamics Companions

- 76 -

www.blindsquirrelpublishing.com
© 2019 Blind Squirrel Publishing, LLC , All Rights Reserved

BLIND SQUIRREL
PUBLISHING

DYNAMICS COMPANIONS
BARE BONES CONFIGURATION GUIDE

CONFIGURING PRODUCT INFORMATION MANAGEMENT WITHIN DYNAMICS 365 FOR FINANCE & OPERATIONS
MODULE 2: CONFIGURING PRODUCTS & SERVICES

Importing Products Using The Data Import Export Framework

How to do it...

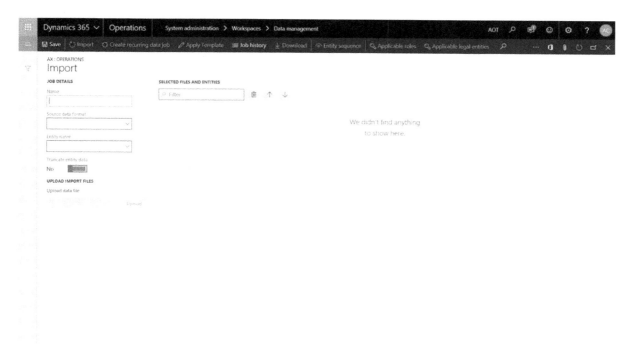

Step 17: Click Import

This will take us to the **Import** project page.

dyn c
www.dynamicscompanions.com
Dynamics Companions

- 77 -

www.blindsquirrelpublishing.com
© 2019 Blind Squirrel Publishing, LLC , All Rights Reserved

BLIND SQUIRREL
PUBLISHING

DYNAMICS COMPANIONS
BARE BONES CONFIGURATION GUIDE

CONFIGURING PRODUCT INFORMATION MANAGEMENT WITHIN DYNAMICS 365 FOR FINANCE & OPERATIONS
MODULE 2: CONFIGURING PRODUCTS & SERVICES

Importing Products Using The Data Import Export Framework

How to do it...

Step 18: Update the Name

The first thing that we will want to do is to give our project a job name.

To do this we will just need to update the **Name** value.

For this example, we will want to set the **Name** to **ReleasedProductImport**.

www.dynamicscompanions.com
Dynamics Companions

- 78 -

www.blindsquirrelpublishing.com
© 2019 Blind Squirrel Publishing, LLC , All Rights Reserved

BLIND SQUIRREL
PUBLISHING

DYNAMICS COMPANIONS
BARE BONES CONFIGURATION GUIDE

CONFIGURING PRODUCT INFORMATION MANAGEMENT WITHIN DYNAMICS 365 FOR FINANCE & OPERATIONS
MODULE 2: CONFIGURING PRODUCTS & SERVICES

Importing Products Using The Data Import Export Framework

How to do it...

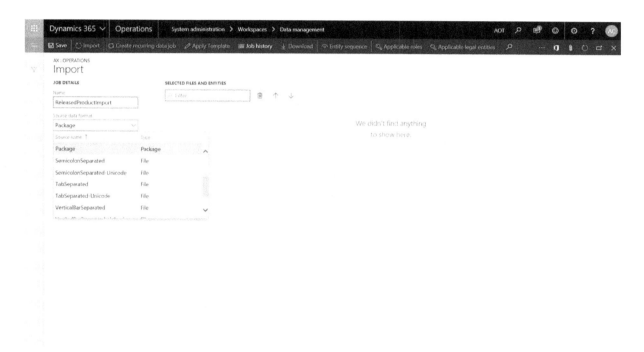

Step 19: Select the Source data format

Now we will want to select the type of source data that we will be importing.

To do this we will just need to select the **Source data format** from the dropdown list.

For this example, even though the data itself if an Excel file, the import file is actually a package, so we will want to click on the **Source data format** dropdown list and select **Package**.

www.dynamicscompanions.com
Dynamics Companions

- 79 -

www.blindsquirrelpublishing.com
© 2019 Blind Squirrel Publishing, LLC , All Rights Reserved

BLIND SQUIRREL
PUBLISHING

DYNAMICS COMPANIONS
BARE BONES CONFIGURATION GUIDE

CONFIGURING PRODUCT INFORMATION MANAGEMENT WITHIN DYNAMICS 365 FOR FINANCE & OPERATIONS
MODULE 2: CONFIGURING PRODUCTS & SERVICES

Importing Products Using The Data Import Export Framework

How to do it...

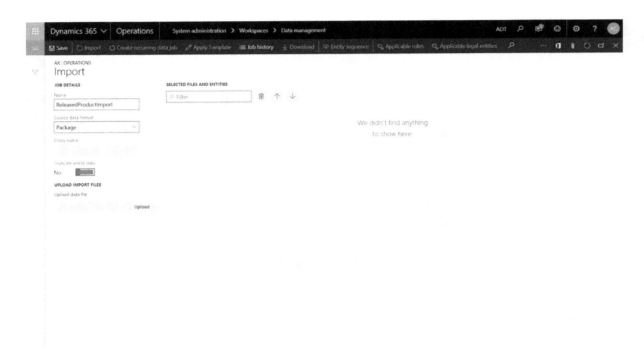

Step 20: Click Upload

Now we will want to add our data package to the project.

To do this just click on the **Upload** button.

www.dynamicscompanions.com
Dynamics Companions

- 80 -

www.blindsquirrelpublishing.com
© 2019 Blind Squirrel Publishing, LLC , All Rights Reserved

BLIND SQUIRREL
PUBLISHING

DYNAMICS COMPANIONS
BARE BONES CONFIGURATION GUIDE

CONFIGURING PRODUCT INFORMATION MANAGEMENT WITHIN DYNAMICS 365 FOR FINANCE & OPERATIONS
MODULE 2: CONFIGURING PRODUCTS & SERVICES

Importing Products Using The Data Import Export Framework

How to do it...

Step 20: Click Upload

This will open up the file explorer and we should be able to see the data packages.

All we need to do here is select the data package that we want to use.

To do this, just select the import package and then click on the **Open** button.

dyn c

www.dynamicscompanions.com
Dynamics Companions

- 81 -

www.blindsquirrelpublishing.com
© 2019 Blind Squirrel Publishing, LLC , All Rights Reserved

BLIND SQUIRREL
PUBLISHING

DYNAMICS COMPANIONS
BARE BONES CONFIGURATION GUIDE

CONFIGURING PRODUCT INFORMATION MANAGEMENT WITHIN DYNAMICS 365 FOR FINANCE & OPERATIONS
MODULE 2: CONFIGURING PRODUCTS & SERVICES

Importing Products Using The Data Import Export Framework

How to do it...

Step 21: Click Import

This will start a process where the data management looks at the file and makes sure that it is in the right format, and within a couple of seconds, the package will show up in the selected entities.

Now all that is left is to start the import process.

To do this just click on the **Import** button in the menu bar.

www.dynamicscompanions.com
Dynamics Companions

- 82 -

www.blindsquirrelpublishing.com
© 2019 Blind Squirrel Publishing, LLC , All Rights Reserved

BLIND SQUIRREL
PUBLISHING

DYNAMICS COMPANIONS
BARE BONES CONFIGURATION GUIDE

CONFIGURING PRODUCT INFORMATION MANAGEMENT WITHIN DYNAMICS 365 FOR FINANCE & OPERATIONS
MODULE 2: CONFIGURING PRODUCTS & SERVICES

Importing Products Using The Data Import Export Framework

How to do it...

Step 22: Click Close

This will open up a dialog box telling us that the import job is being submitted to the queue.

We can dismiss this dialog.

To do this just click on the **Close** button.

dyn
www.dynamicscompanions.com
Dynamics Companions
- 83 -
www.blindsquirrelpublishing.com
© 2019 Blind Squirrel Publishing, LLC , All Rights Reserved
BLIND SQUIRREL
PUBLISHING

DYNAMICS COMPANIONS
BARE BONES CONFIGURATION GUIDE

CONFIGURING PRODUCT INFORMATION MANAGEMENT WITHIN DYNAMICS 365 FOR FINANCE & OPERATIONS
MODULE 2: CONFIGURING PRODUCTS & SERVICES

Importing Products Using The Data Import Export Framework

How to do it...

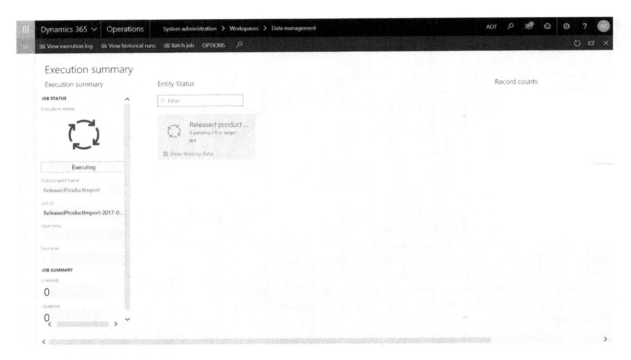

Step 23: Click Refresh

Then we will be taken to the **Execution summary** form where we can see the progress of the import.

All we need to do is wait for the import to process and maybe refresh the form.

To do this just click on the **Refresh** icon.

www.dynamicscompanions.com
Dynamics Companions

- 84 -

www.blindsquirrelpublishing.com
© 2019 Blind Squirrel Publishing, LLC , All Rights Reserved

BLIND SQUIRREL
PUBLISHING

DYNAMICS COMPANIONS
BARE BONES CONFIGURATION GUIDE

CONFIGURING PRODUCT INFORMATION MANAGEMENT WITHIN DYNAMICS 365 FOR FINANCE & OPERATIONS
MODULE 2: CONFIGURING PRODUCTS & SERVICES

Importing Products Using The Data Import Export Framework

How to do it...

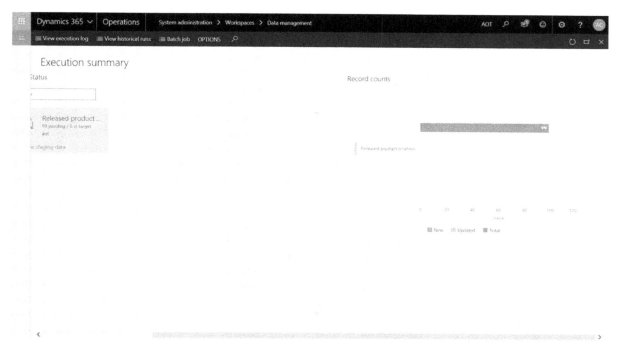

Step 23: Click Refresh

After a little bit, we will see that all of the products have been moved into the staging tables.

www.dynamicscompanions.com
Dynamics Companions

- 85 -

www.blindsquirrelpublishing.com
© 2019 Blind Squirrel Publishing, LLC , All Rights Reserved

BLIND SQUIRREL
PUBLISHING

DYNAMICS COMPANIONS
BARE BONES CONFIGURATION GUIDE

CONFIGURING PRODUCT INFORMATION MANAGEMENT WITHIN DYNAMICS 365 FOR FINANCE & OPERATIONS
MODULE 2: CONFIGURING PRODUCTS & SERVICES

Importing Products Using The Data Import Export Framework

How to do it...

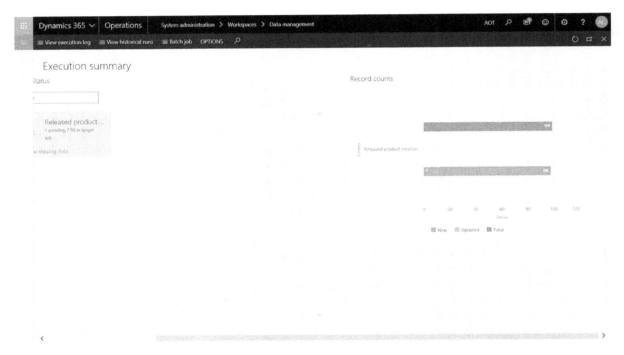

Step 23: Click Refresh

And then a little while later we will also see that all of the products have been moved into the **Released products** table.

dync

www.dynamicscompanions.com
Dynamics Companions

- 86 -

www.blindsquirrelpublishing.com
© 2019 Blind Squirrel Publishing, LLC , All Rights Reserved

BLIND SQUIRREL
PUBLISHING

DYNAMICS COMPANIONS
BARE BONES CONFIGURATION GUIDE

CONFIGURING PRODUCT INFORMATION MANAGEMENT WITHIN DYNAMICS 365 FOR FINANCE & OPERATIONS
MODULE 2: CONFIGURING PRODUCTS & SERVICES

Importing Products Using The Data Import Export Framework

How to do it...

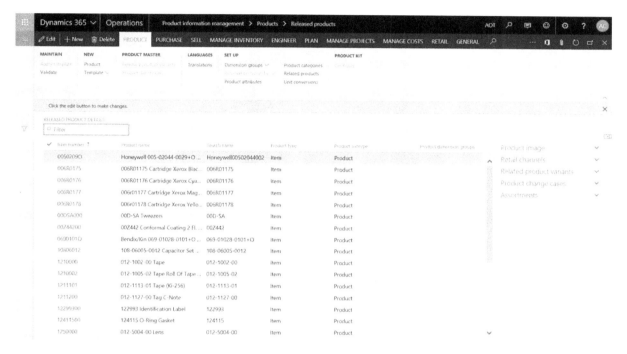

Step 24: Open the Released products form through the menu

If you don't believe it, then just open up the **Released products** form.

To do this, open up the navigation panel, expand out the **Modules** and group, and click on **Product information management** to see all of the menu items that are available. Then click on the **Released products** menu item within the **Products** group.

We will see that all of the products form the import file are now there.

dync
www.dynamicscompanions.com
Dynamics Companions

- 87 -

www.blindsquirrelpublishing.com
© 2019 Blind Squirrel Publishing, LLC , All Rights Reserved

BLIND SQUIRREL
PUBLISHING

DYNAMICS COMPANIONS
BARE BONES CONFIGURATION GUIDE

CONFIGURING PRODUCT INFORMATION MANAGEMENT WITHIN DYNAMICS 365 FOR FINANCE & OPERATIONS
MODULE 2: CONFIGURING PRODUCTS & SERVICES

Importing Products Using The Data Import Export Framework

How to do it...

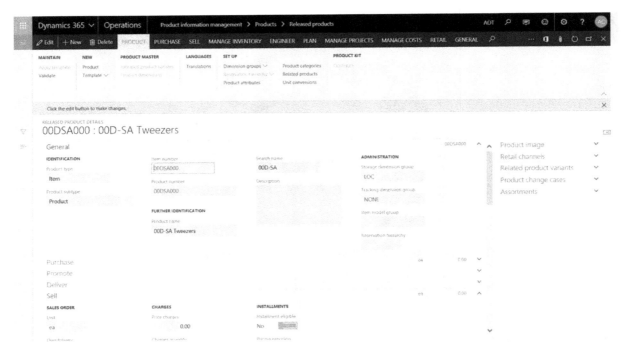

Step 24: Open the Released products form through the menu

If we open up any of the products as well, we will see that some of the key information is already loaded for us – like the **Purchase** and **Sales** prices.

www.dynamicscompanions.com
Dynamics Companions

- 88 -

www.blindsquirrelpublishing.com
© 2019 Blind Squirrel Publishing, LLC , All Rights Reserved

BLIND SQUIRREL
PUBLISHING

DYNAMICS COMPANIONS
BARE BONES CONFIGURATION GUIDE

CONFIGURING PRODUCT INFORMATION MANAGEMENT WITHIN DYNAMICS 365 FOR FINANCE & OPERATIONS
MODULE 2: CONFIGURING PRODUCTS & SERVICES

Importing Products Using The Data Import Export Framework

Review

Now that was easy!

DYNAMICS COMPANIONS
BARE BONES CONFIGURATION GUIDE

CONFIGURING PRODUCT INFORMATION MANAGEMENT WITHIN DYNAMICS 365 FOR FINANCE & OPERATIONS
MODULE 2: CONFIGURING PRODUCTS & SERVICES

Summary

In this section we have shown how you are able to create products a number of different ways, including by hand, and also through the import functions.

DYNAMICS COMPANIONS
BARE BONES CONFIGURATION GUIDE

CONFIGURING PRODUCT INFORMATION MANAGEMENT WITHIN DYNAMICS 365 FOR FINANCE & OPERATIONS
MODULE 2: CONFIGURING PRODUCTS & SERVICES

Creating A Service Item

The products that we have been creating up until now have been physical items, but that doesn't mean that is the only type that you can use. You can also create **Service** products as well which bypass all of the inventory tracking and physical requirements of the tangible products.

Topics Covered

- Opening the Releases products form

- Creating a Service Released Product

- Summary

DYNAMICS COMPANIONS
BARE BONES CONFIGURATION GUIDE

CONFIGURING PRODUCT INFORMATION MANAGEMENT WITHIN DYNAMICS 365 FOR FINANCE & OPERATIONS
MODULE 2: CONFIGURING PRODUCTS & SERVICES

Opening the Releases products form

We will create a Service product pretty much the same way as we create any of the other products.

To do this we will need to return to the **Released products** maintenance form.

How to do it...

Step 1: Open the Released products form through the menu

We can get to the **Released products** form a couple of different ways. The first way is through the master menu.

Navigate to Product information management > Products > Released products

Step 2: Open the Released products form through the menu search

Another way that we can find the **Released products** form is through the menu search feature.

Type in **released products** into the menu search and select **Released products**

That will open up the **Released product details** list page where we will be able to see all of the products that we have already set up.

Now we will create a simple service item.

DYNAMICS COMPANIONS
BARE BONES CONFIGURATION GUIDE

CONFIGURING PRODUCT INFORMATION MANAGEMENT WITHIN DYNAMICS 365 FOR FINANCE & OPERATIONS
MODULE 2: CONFIGURING PRODUCTS & SERVICES

Opening the Releases products form

How to do it...

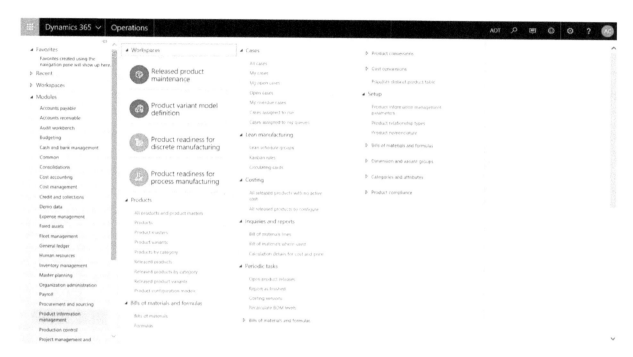

Step 1: Open the Released products form through the menu

We can get to the **Released products** form a couple of different ways. The first way is through the master menu.

To do this, open up the navigation panel, expand out the **Modules** and group, and click on **Product information management** to see all of the menu items that are available. Then click on the **Released products** menu item within the **Products** group.

www.dynamicscompanions.com
Dynamics Companions

- 93 -

www.blindsquirrelpublishing.com
© 2019 Blind Squirrel Publishing, LLC , All Rights Reserved

BLIND SQUIRREL
PUBLISHING

DYNAMICS COMPANIONS
BARE BONES CONFIGURATION GUIDE

CONFIGURING PRODUCT INFORMATION MANAGEMENT WITHIN DYNAMICS 365 FOR FINANCE & OPERATIONS
MODULE 2: CONFIGURING PRODUCTS & SERVICES

Opening the Releases products form

How to do it...

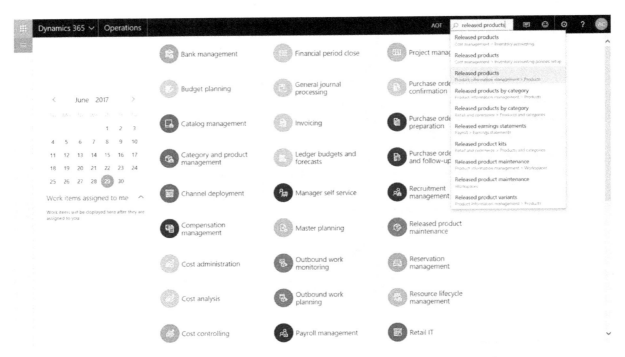

Step 2: Open the Released products form through the menu search

Another way that we can find the **Released products** form is through the menu search feature.

We can do this by clicking on the search icon in the header of the form (or by pressing **ALT+G**) and then type in **released products** storage into the search box. Then you will be able to select the **Released products** form from the dropdown list.

DYNAMICS COMPANIONS
BARE BONES CONFIGURATION GUIDE

CONFIGURING PRODUCT INFORMATION MANAGEMENT WITHIN DYNAMICS 365 FOR FINANCE & OPERATIONS
MODULE 2: CONFIGURING PRODUCTS & SERVICES

Opening the Releases products form

How to do it...

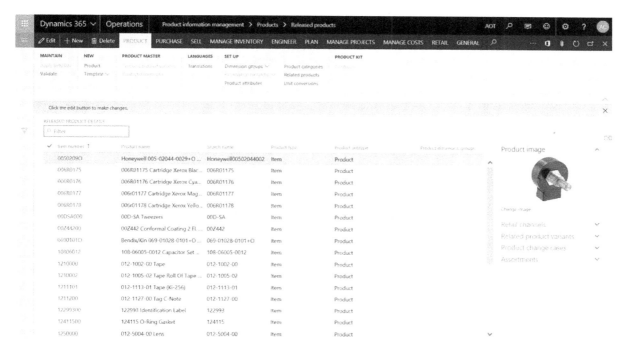

Step 2: Open the Released products form through the menu search

That will open up the **Released product details** list page where we will be able to see all of the products that we have already set up.

Now we will create a simple service item.

www.dynamicscompanions.com
Dynamics Companions

- 95 -

www.blindsquirrelpublishing.com
© 2019 Blind Squirrel Publishing, LLC , All Rights Reserved

BLIND SQUIRREL
PUBLISHING

DYNAMICS COMPANIONS
BARE BONES CONFIGURATION GUIDE

CONFIGURING PRODUCT INFORMATION MANAGEMENT WITHIN DYNAMICS 365 FOR FINANCE & OPERATIONS
MODULE 2: CONFIGURING PRODUCTS & SERVICES

Creating a Service Released Product

Now we will want to create a new released product record, but for this product we will make it a service rather than an item.

How to do it...

Step 1: Click Product

That will open up the **Released product details** list page where we will be able to see all of the products that we have already set up.

Now we will create a simple service item.

Click on the **Product** button within the **New** group of the **PRODUCTS** action bar.

This will open up the **New Released Product** dialog box that you used in the previous example.

Step 2: Select the Product type

Now we will want to change the type of product that we are creating from an **Item** to a **Service.**

Click on the **Product type** dropdown list and select **Service**

Step 3: Update the Product number

Now we will want to give our service a product number to identify it.

Set the Product number to DIAG-1001

Step 4: Update the Product name

The next step is to give the service a name that explains the service a little better than the product number.

Set the Product name to Diagnostic Service

Step 5: Update the Search name

Now we will want to give our Service product a name that we can use to search for it with.

Set the Search name to DiagnosticService

Step 6: Select the Inventory unit

Now that we have specified the item number and names we will want to move on and tell the system the units that we want to track the service in.

We will start by selecting a default unit to track the service inventory in.

Click on the **Inventory unit** dropdown list and select **hr**

Step 7: Select the Purchase unit

Now we will want to select the unit that we will purchase the service item in.

Click on the **Purchase unit** dropdown list and select **hr**

Step 8: Select the Sales unit

And finally we will want to select the unit that we will want to sell the service in.

DYNAMICS COMPANIONS
BARE BONES CONFIGURATION GUIDE

CONFIGURING PRODUCT INFORMATION MANAGEMENT WITHIN DYNAMICS 365 FOR FINANCE & OPERATIONS
MODULE 2: CONFIGURING PRODUCTS & SERVICES

Click on the **Sales unit** dropdown list and select **hr.**

Step 9: Click OK

Now that we have specified all of the key fields for the service we can create the item.

Click on the **OK** button.

When we return back to the **Released Products** list page we will see that we now have a Service item.

If we open up the record then we can update it just the same way as we did for a physical product.

www.dynamicscompanions.com
Dynamics Companions

- 97 -

www.blindsquirrelpublishing.com
© 2019 Blind Squirrel Publishing, LLC , All Rights Reserved

BLIND SQUIRREL
PUBLISHING

DYNAMICS COMPANIONS
BARE BONES CONFIGURATION GUIDE

CONFIGURING PRODUCT INFORMATION MANAGEMENT WITHIN DYNAMICS 365 FOR FINANCE & OPERATIONS
MODULE 2: CONFIGURING PRODUCTS & SERVICES

Creating a Service Released Product

How to do it...

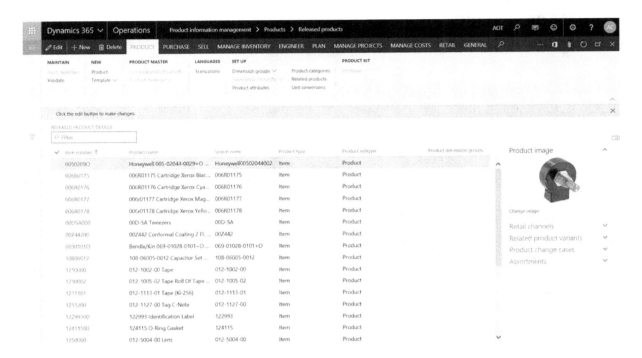

Step 1: Click Product

That will open up the **Released product details** list page where we will be able to see all of the products that we have already set up.

Now we will create a simple service item.

To do this just click on the **Product** button within the **New** group of the **PRODUCTS** action bar.

www.dynamicscompanions.com
Dynamics Companions

- 98 -

www.blindsquirrelpublishing.com
© 2019 Blind Squirrel Publishing, LLC , All Rights Reserved

BLIND SQUIRREL
PUBLISHING

DYNAMICS COMPANIONS
BARE BONES CONFIGURATION GUIDE

CONFIGURING PRODUCT INFORMATION MANAGEMENT WITHIN DYNAMICS 365 FOR FINANCE & OPERATIONS
MODULE 2: CONFIGURING PRODUCTS & SERVICES

Creating a Service Released Product

How to do it...

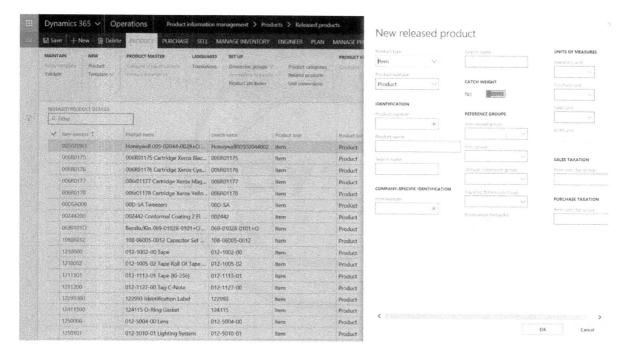

Step 1: Click Product

This will open up the **New Released Product** dialog box that you used in the previous example.

dyn c

www.dynamicscompanions.com
Dynamics Companions

- 99 -

www.blindsquirrelpublishing.com
© 2019 Blind Squirrel Publishing, LLC , All Rights Reserved

BLIND SQUIRREL
PUBLISHING

DYNAMICS COMPANIONS
BARE BONES CONFIGURATION GUIDE

CONFIGURING PRODUCT INFORMATION MANAGEMENT WITHIN DYNAMICS 365 FOR FINANCE & OPERATIONS
MODULE 2: CONFIGURING PRODUCTS & SERVICES

Creating a Service Released Product

How to do it...

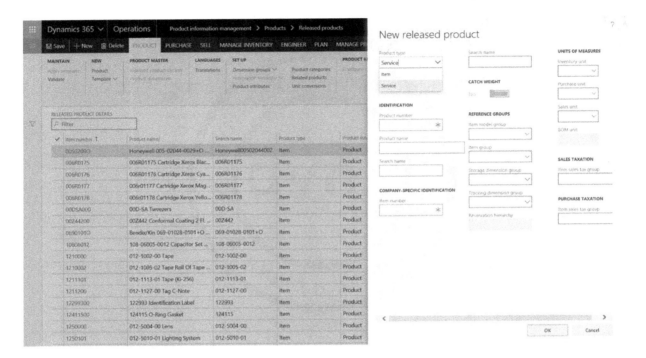

Step 2: Select the Product type

Now we will want to change the type of product that we are creating from an **Item** to a **Service**.

To do this we will just need to select the **Product type** from the dropdown list.

For this example, we will want to click on the **Product type** dropdown list and select **Service**.

dyn c

www.dynamicscompanions.com
Dynamics Companions

- 100 -

www.blindsquirrelpublishing.com
© 2019 Blind Squirrel Publishing, LLC , All Rights Reserved

BLIND SQUIRREL
PUBLISHING

DYNAMICS COMPANIONS
BARE BONES CONFIGURATION GUIDE

CONFIGURING PRODUCT INFORMATION MANAGEMENT WITHIN DYNAMICS 365 FOR FINANCE & OPERATIONS
MODULE 2: CONFIGURING PRODUCTS & SERVICES

Creating a Service Released Product

How to do it...

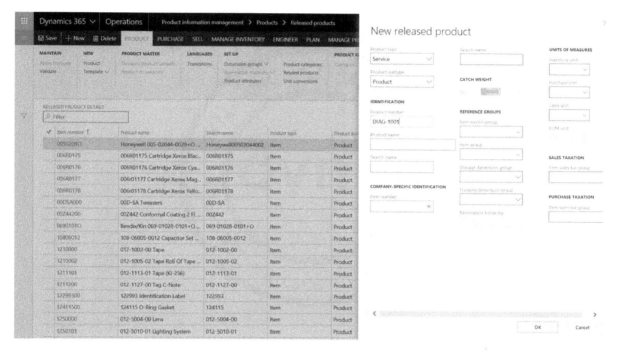

Step 3: Update the Product number

Now we will want to give our service a product number to identify it.

To do this we will just need to update the **Product number** value.

For this example, we will want to set the **Product number** to **DIAG-1001**.

www.dynamicscompanions.com
Dynamics Companions

- 101 -

www.blindsquirrelpublishing.com
© 2019 Blind Squirrel Publishing, LLC , All Rights Reserved

BLIND SQUIRREL
PUBLISHING

DYNAMICS COMPANIONS
BARE BONES CONFIGURATION GUIDE

CONFIGURING PRODUCT INFORMATION MANAGEMENT WITHIN DYNAMICS 365 FOR FINANCE & OPERATIONS
MODULE 2: CONFIGURING PRODUCTS & SERVICES

Creating a Service Released Product

How to do it...

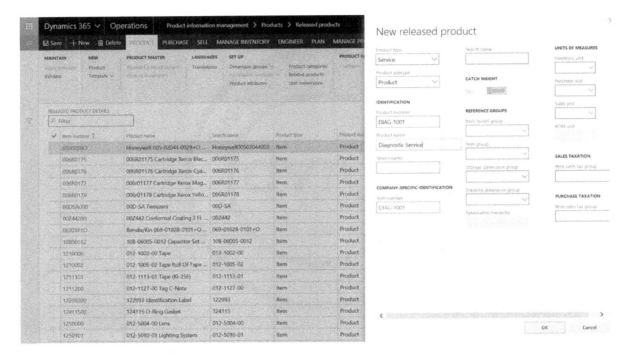

Step 4: Update the Product name

The next step is to give the service a name that explains the service a little better than the product number.

To do this we will just need to update the **Product name** value.

For this example, we will want to set the **Product name** to **Diagnostic Service**.

www.dynamicscompanions.com
Dynamics Companions

- 102 -

www.blindsquirrelpublishing.com
© 2019 Blind Squirrel Publishing, LLC , All Rights Reserved

BLIND SQUIRREL
PUBLISHING

DYNAMICS COMPANIONS
BARE BONES CONFIGURATION GUIDE

CONFIGURING PRODUCT INFORMATION MANAGEMENT WITHIN DYNAMICS 365 FOR FINANCE & OPERATIONS
MODULE 2: CONFIGURING PRODUCTS & SERVICES

Creating a Service Released Product

How to do it...

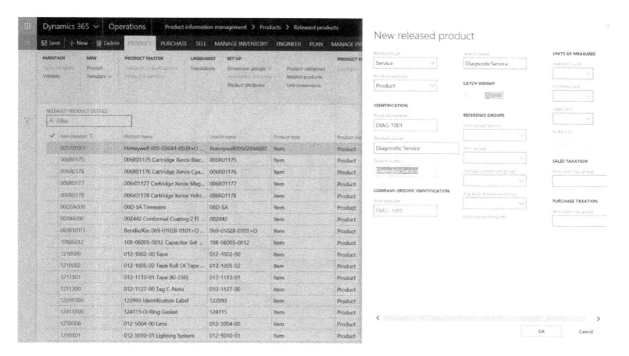

Step 5: Update the Search name

Now we will want to give our Service product a name that we can use to search for it with.

To do this we will just need to update the **Search name** value.

For this example, we will want to set the **Search name** to **DiagnosticService**.

www.dynamicscompanions.com
Dynamics Companions

- 103 -

www.blindsquirrelpublishing.com
© 2019 Blind Squirrel Publishing, LLC , All Rights Reserved

BLIND SQUIRREL
PUBLISHING

DYNAMICS COMPANIONS
BARE BONES CONFIGURATION GUIDE

CONFIGURING PRODUCT INFORMATION MANAGEMENT WITHIN DYNAMICS 365 FOR FINANCE & OPERATIONS
MODULE 2: CONFIGURING PRODUCTS & SERVICES

Creating a Service Released Product

How to do it...

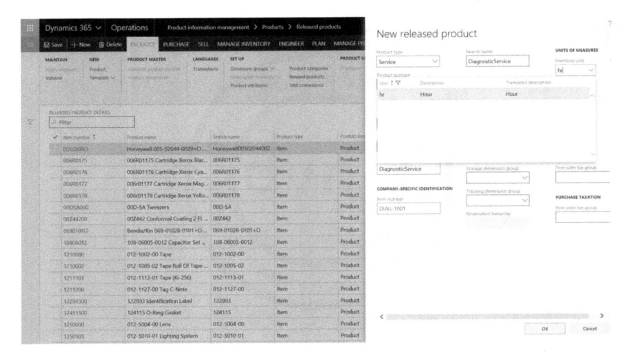

Step 6: Select the Inventory unit

Now that we have specified the item number and names we will want to move on and tell the system the units that we want to track the service in.

We will start by selecting a default unit to track the service inventory in.

To do this we will just need to select the **Inventory unit** from the dropdown list.

For this example, we will want to click on the **Inventory unit** dropdown list and select **hr**.

www.dynamicscompanions.com
Dynamics Companions

- 104 -

www.blindsquirrelpublishing.com
© 2019 Blind Squirrel Publishing, LLC , All Rights Reserved

BLIND SQUIRREL
PUBLISHING

DYNAMICS COMPANIONS
BARE BONES CONFIGURATION GUIDE

CONFIGURING PRODUCT INFORMATION MANAGEMENT WITHIN DYNAMICS 365 FOR FINANCE & OPERATIONS
MODULE 2: CONFIGURING PRODUCTS & SERVICES

Creating a Service Released Product

How to do it...

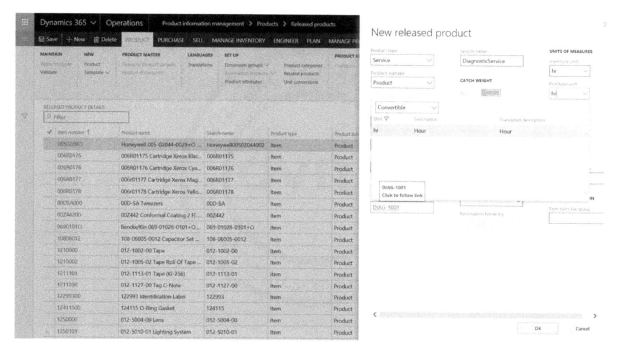

Step 7: Select the Purchase unit

Now we will want to select the unit that we will purchase the service item in.

To do this we will just need to select the **Purchase unit** from the dropdown list.

For this example, we will want to click on the **Purchase unit** dropdown list and select **hr**.

www.dynamicscompanions.com
Dynamics Companions

- 105 -

www.blindsquirrelpublishing.com
© 2019 Blind Squirrel Publishing, LLC , All Rights Reserved

BLIND SQUIRREL
PUBLISHING

DYNAMICS COMPANIONS
BARE BONES CONFIGURATION GUIDE

CONFIGURING PRODUCT INFORMATION MANAGEMENT WITHIN DYNAMICS 365 FOR FINANCE & OPERATIONS
MODULE 2: CONFIGURING PRODUCTS & SERVICES

Creating a Service Released Product

How to do it...

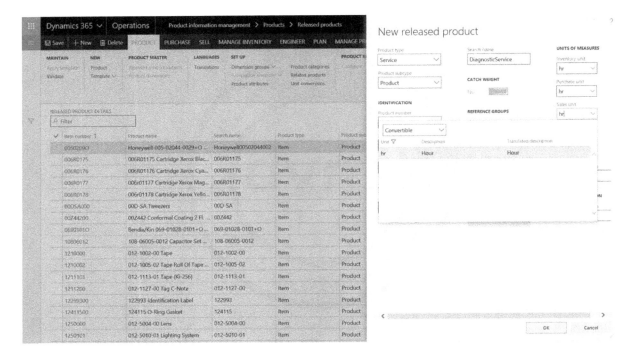

Step 8: Select the Sales unit

And finally we will want to select the unit that we will want to sell the service in.

To do this we will just need to select the **Sales unit** from the dropdown list.

For this example, we will want to sell the service as time and will click on the **Sales unit** dropdown list and select **hr**.

dyn

www.dynamicscompanions.com
Dynamics Companions

- 106 -

www.blindsquirrelpublishing.com
© 2019 Blind Squirrel Publishing, LLC , All Rights Reserved

BLIND SQUIRREL
PUBLISHING

DYNAMICS COMPANIONS
BARE BONES CONFIGURATION GUIDE

CONFIGURING PRODUCT INFORMATION MANAGEMENT WITHIN DYNAMICS 365 FOR FINANCE & OPERATIONS
MODULE 2: CONFIGURING PRODUCTS & SERVICES

Creating a Service Released Product

How to do it...

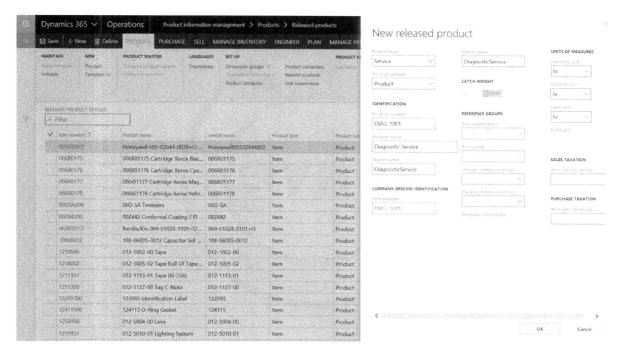

Step 9: Click OK

Now that we have specified all of the key fields for the service we can create the item.

To do this just click on the **OK** button.

www.dynamicscompanions.com
Dynamics Companions

- 107 -

www.blindsquirrelpublishing.com
© 2019 Blind Squirrel Publishing, LLC , All Rights Reserved

BLIND SQUIRREL
PUBLISHING

DYNAMICS COMPANIONS
BARE BONES CONFIGURATION GUIDE

CONFIGURING PRODUCT INFORMATION MANAGEMENT WITHIN DYNAMICS 365 FOR FINANCE & OPERATIONS
MODULE 2: CONFIGURING PRODUCTS & SERVICES

Creating a Service Released Product

How to do it...

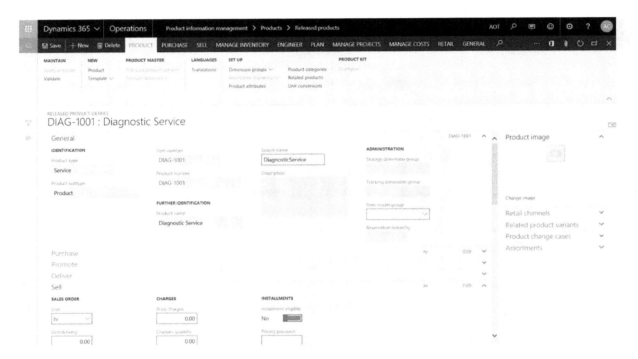

Step 9: Click OK

When we return back to the **Released Products** list page we will see that we now have a Service item.

If we open up the record then we can update it just the same way as we did for a physical product.

How easy is that?

www.dynamicscompanions.com
Dynamics Companions

- 108 -

www.blindsquirrelpublishing.com
© 2019 Blind Squirrel Publishing, LLC , All Rights Reserved

BLIND SQUIRREL
PUBLISHING

DYNAMICS COMPANIONS
BARE BONES CONFIGURATION GUIDE

CONFIGURING PRODUCT INFORMATION MANAGEMENT WITHIN DYNAMICS 365 FOR FINANCE & OPERATIONS
MODULE 2: CONFIGURING PRODUCTS & SERVICES

Summary

As you can see, Service items are not that much different from the tangible products that we created in the previous section. The major difference is that we don't have to worry about any of the inventory tracking.

www.dynamicscompanions.com
Dynamics Companions

- 109 -

www.blindsquirrelpublishing.com
© 2019 Blind Squirrel Publishing, LLC , All Rights Reserved

BLIND SQUIRREL
PUBLISHING

DYNAMICS COMPANIONS
BARE BONES CONFIGURATION GUIDE

CONFIGURING PRODUCT INFORMATION MANAGEMENT WITHIN DYNAMICS 365 FOR FINANCE & OPERATIONS
MODULE 2: CONFIGURING PRODUCTS & SERVICES

Creating Product Templates

If you have products that are almost the same in their configurations except for some small tweaks here and there, then you can save a little bit of time by creating a master template for the products from one that is already set up and then use it when you create new products.

Topics Covered

- Creating a Template from a Released Product

- Creating New Products Using Product Templates

- Applying Templates In Bulk to Multiple Records

- Updating Product Details Using The Edit In Grid Function

- Summary

DYNAMICS COMPANIONS
BARE BONES CONFIGURATION GUIDE

CONFIGURING PRODUCT INFORMATION MANAGEMENT WITHIN DYNAMICS 365 FOR FINANCE & OPERATIONS
MODULE 2: CONFIGURING PRODUCTS & SERVICES

Creating a Template from a Released Product

Creating templates are easy. All we need to do is find the product that we want to use as the example and then create the template from it.

How to do it...

Step 1: Open the Released products form through the menu

We will start off my opening up the **Released Product** record that is going to be used as the master for the template.

Navigate to Product information management > Products > Released products and select a product record.

This will open up the details of the **Released product** that we will want to turn into a template.

Step 2: Click on Create Personal Template

Now we will want to create a template from the record.

Click on the **Template** button within the **New** group of the **Product** ribbon bar, and select the **Create Personal Template**

This will open up a **Create Template** dialog box.

Step 3: Update the Name

Now we will want to give our template a name so that we can identify it.

Set the Name to Capacitor Sets

Step 4: Update the Description

And next we will want to add a more detailed description for the template.

Set the Description to Capacitor Set Template

Step 5: Click OK

Now we can create the template record.

Click on the **OK** button.

After we have done that, we will be returned back to the **Released product** page and we will be done.

DYNAMICS COMPANIONS
BARE BONES CONFIGURATION GUIDE

CONFIGURING PRODUCT INFORMATION MANAGEMENT WITHIN DYNAMICS 365 FOR FINANCE & OPERATIONS
MODULE 2: CONFIGURING PRODUCTS & SERVICES

Creating a Template from a Released Product

How to do it...

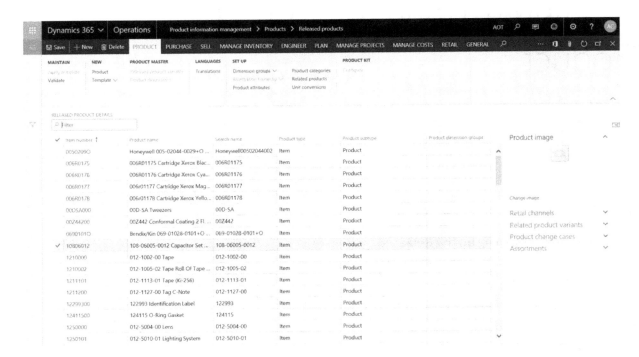

Step 1: Open the Released products form through the menu

We will start off my opening up the **Released Product** record that is going to be used as the master for the template.

To do this, open up the navigation panel, expand out the **Modules** and group, and click on **Product information management** to see all of the menu items that are available. Then click on the **Released products** menu item within the **Products** group.

When the **Released products** list page is displayed we just need to select the product that we want to use as the template.

For this example we will select the **10806012** product.

www.dynamicscompanions.com
Dynamics Companions

- 112 -

www.blindsquirrelpublishing.com
© 2019 Blind Squirrel Publishing, LLC , All Rights Reserved

BLIND SQUIRREL
PUBLISHING

DYNAMICS COMPANIONS
BARE BONES CONFIGURATION GUIDE

CONFIGURING PRODUCT INFORMATION MANAGEMENT WITHIN DYNAMICS 365 FOR FINANCE & OPERATIONS
MODULE 2: CONFIGURING PRODUCTS & SERVICES

Creating a Template from a Released Product

How to do it...

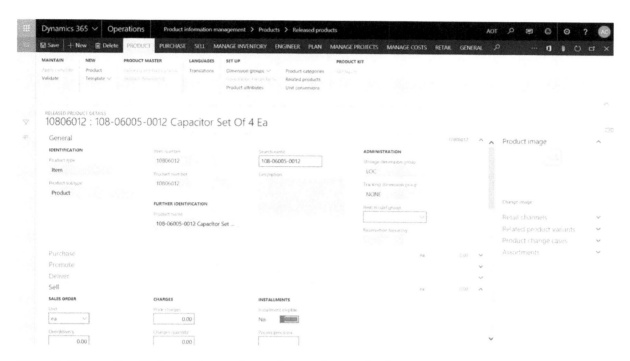

Step 1: Open the Released products form through the menu

This will open up the details of the **Released product** that we will want to turn into a template.

dyn c

www.dynamicscompanions.com
Dynamics Companions

- 113 -

www.blindsquirrelpublishing.com
© 2019 Blind Squirrel Publishing, LLC , All Rights Reserved

BLIND SQUIRREL
PUBLISHING

DYNAMICS COMPANIONS
BARE BONES CONFIGURATION GUIDE

CONFIGURING PRODUCT INFORMATION MANAGEMENT WITHIN DYNAMICS 365 FOR FINANCE & OPERATIONS
MODULE 2: CONFIGURING PRODUCTS & SERVICES

Creating a Template from a Released Product

How to do it...

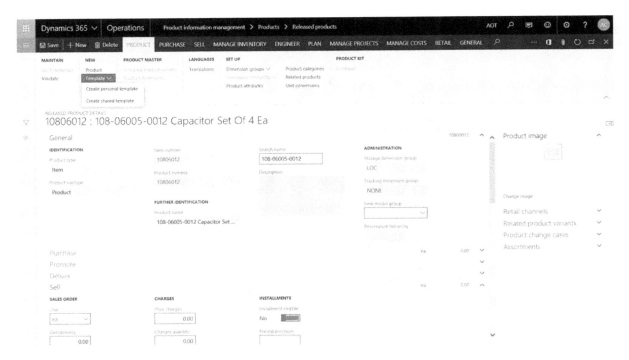

Step 2: Click on Create Personal Template

Now we will want to create a template from the record.

To do this we just click on the **Template** button within the **New** group of the **Product** ribbon bar, and select the **Create Personal Template**.

If you want to share the template with everyone else then you can select the **Create Shared Template**.

www.dynamicscompanions.com
Dynamics Companions

- 114 -

www.blindsquirrelpublishing.com
© 2019 Blind Squirrel Publishing, LLC , All Rights Reserved

BLIND SQUIRREL
PUBLISHING

DYNAMICS COMPANIONS
BARE BONES CONFIGURATION GUIDE

CONFIGURING PRODUCT INFORMATION MANAGEMENT WITHIN DYNAMICS 365 FOR FINANCE & OPERATIONS
MODULE 2: CONFIGURING PRODUCTS & SERVICES

Creating a Template from a Released Product

How to do it...

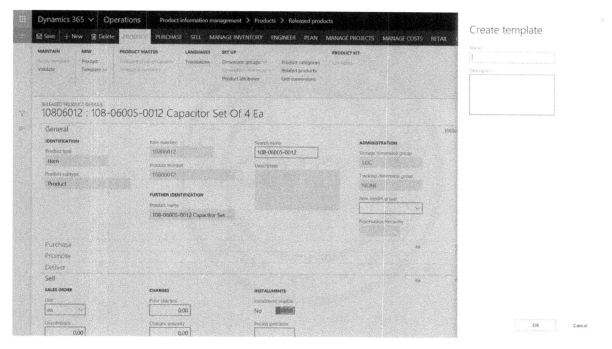

Step 2: Click on Create Personal Template

This will open up a **Create Template** dialog box.

www.dynamicscompanions.com
Dynamics Companions

- 115 -

www.blindsquirrelpublishing.com
© 2019 Blind Squirrel Publishing, LLC , All Rights Reserved

BLIND SQUIRREL
PUBLISHING

DYNAMICS COMPANIONS
BARE BONES CONFIGURATION GUIDE

CONFIGURING PRODUCT INFORMATION MANAGEMENT WITHIN DYNAMICS 365 FOR FINANCE & OPERATIONS
MODULE 2: CONFIGURING PRODUCTS & SERVICES

Creating a Template from a Released Product

How to do it...

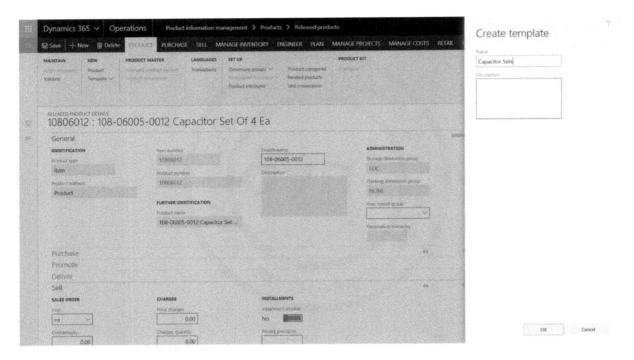

Step 3: Update the Name

Now we will want to give our template a name so that we can identify it.

To do this we will just need to update the **Name** value.

For this example, we will want to set the **Name** to **Capacitor Sets**.

www.dynamicscompanions.com
Dynamics Companions

- 116 -

www.blindsquirrelpublishing.com
© 2019 Blind Squirrel Publishing, LLC , All Rights Reserved

BLIND SQUIRREL
PUBLISHING

DYNAMICS COMPANIONS
BARE BONES CONFIGURATION GUIDE

CONFIGURING PRODUCT INFORMATION MANAGEMENT WITHIN DYNAMICS 365 FOR FINANCE & OPERATIONS
MODULE 2: CONFIGURING PRODUCTS & SERVICES

Creating a Template from a Released Product

How to do it...

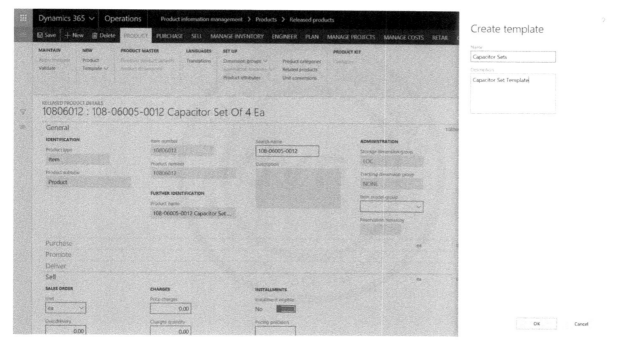

Step 4: Update the Description

And next we will want to add a more detailed description for the template.

To do this we will just need to update the **Description** value.

For this example, we will want to set the **Description** to **Capacitor Set Template**.

www.dynamicscompanions.com
Dynamics Companions

- 117 -

www.blindsquirrelpublishing.com
© 2019 Blind Squirrel Publishing, LLC , All Rights Reserved

BLIND SQUIRREL
PUBLISHING

DYNAMICS COMPANIONS
BARE BONES CONFIGURATION GUIDE

CONFIGURING PRODUCT INFORMATION MANAGEMENT WITHIN DYNAMICS 365 FOR FINANCE & OPERATIONS
MODULE 2: CONFIGURING PRODUCTS & SERVICES

Creating a Template from a Released Product

How to do it...

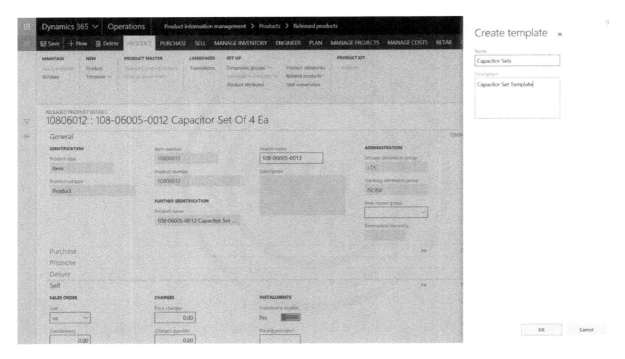

Step 5: Click OK

Now we can create the template record.

To do this just click on the **OK** button.

After we have done that, we will

www.dynamicscompanions.com
Dynamics Companions

- 118 -

www.blindsquirrelpublishing.com
© 2019 Blind Squirrel Publishing, LLC , All Rights Reserved

BLIND SQUIRREL
PUBLISHING

DYNAMICS COMPANIONS
BARE BONES CONFIGURATION GUIDE

CONFIGURING PRODUCT INFORMATION MANAGEMENT WITHIN DYNAMICS 365 FOR FINANCE & OPERATIONS
MODULE 2: CONFIGURING PRODUCTS & SERVICES

Creating a Template from a Released Product

How to do it...

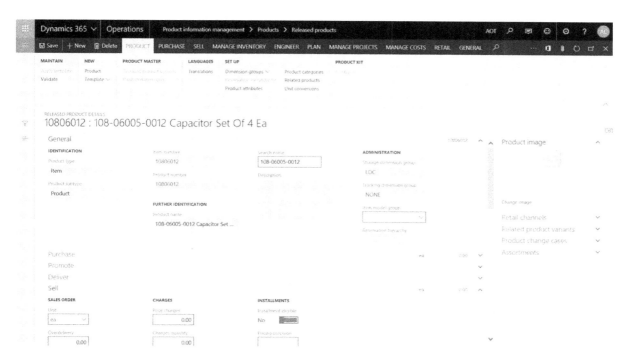

Step 5: Click OK

After we have done that, we will be returned back to the **Released product** page and we will be done.

www.dynamicscompanions.com
Dynamics Companions

- 119 -

www.blindsquirrelpublishing.com
© 2019 Blind Squirrel Publishing, LLC , All Rights Reserved

BLIND SQUIRREL
PUBLISHING

DYNAMICS COMPANIONS
BARE BONES CONFIGURATION GUIDE

CONFIGURING PRODUCT INFORMATION MANAGEMENT WITHIN DYNAMICS 365 FOR FINANCE & OPERATIONS
MODULE 2: CONFIGURING PRODUCTS & SERVICES

Creating New Products Using Product Templates

You can use the templates that you create a couple of different ways. The first that we will look at is the ability to select the template as you are creating the product records, and have all of the template details default in for you.

How to do it...

Step 1: Open the Released products form and click New

To do this we will just want to create a new product just the same way as we did before.

Open the **Released products** form and click on the **New** button.

This will open up the **New released product** panel where we can start specifying our products initial details.

Step 2: Set the Product number Product name and Search name

We will now want to start adding the default codes and descriptions for our new product.

Set the Product number to 10806014, the Product name to 108-06005-0014 Capacitor Set of 4 Ea and the Search name to 108-06005-0014

Step 3: Select the Apply template

You will notice that something is a little different now that you have the templates

created, there is a new field group called **Administration** with a new **Apply template** field.

Now we will want to use one of the templates that we have saved away to default in some more information on the product.

Click on the **Apply template** dropdown list and select **Capacitor Sets**

Step 4: Click OK

This will default in all of the codes that you had configured on the master record for you into this new record.

If everything looks good then we can create the new record.

Click on the **OK** button.

When we return back to the product that we just created we will see that not only have the units been updated, but also the default pricing and any other fields that you may have configured.

www.dynamicscompanions.com
Dynamics Companions

- 120 -

www.blindsquirrelpublishing.com
© 2019 Blind Squirrel Publishing, LLC , All Rights Reserved

BLIND SQUIRREL
PUBLISHING

DYNAMICS COMPANIONS
BARE BONES CONFIGURATION GUIDE

CONFIGURING PRODUCT INFORMATION MANAGEMENT WITHIN DYNAMICS 365 FOR FINANCE & OPERATIONS
MODULE 2: CONFIGURING PRODUCTS & SERVICES

Creating New Products Using Product Templates

How to do it...

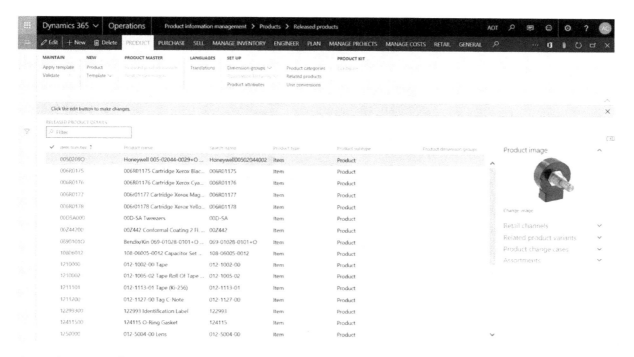

Step 1: Open the Released products form and click New

To do this we will just want to create a new product just the same way as we did before.

To do this, open up the navigation panel, expand out the **Modules** and group, and click on **Product information management** to see all of the menu items that are available. Then click on the **Released Products** menu item within the **Products** group.

Then click on the **New** button in the menu bar.

dyn

www.dynamicscompanions.com
Dynamics Companions

- 121 -

www.blindsquirrelpublishing.com
© 2019 Blind Squirrel Publishing, LLC , All Rights Reserved

BLIND SQUIRREL
PUBLISHING

DYNAMICS COMPANIONS
BARE BONES CONFIGURATION GUIDE

CONFIGURING PRODUCT INFORMATION MANAGEMENT WITHIN DYNAMICS 365 FOR FINANCE & OPERATIONS
MODULE 2: CONFIGURING PRODUCTS & SERVICES

Creating New Products Using Product Templates

How to do it...

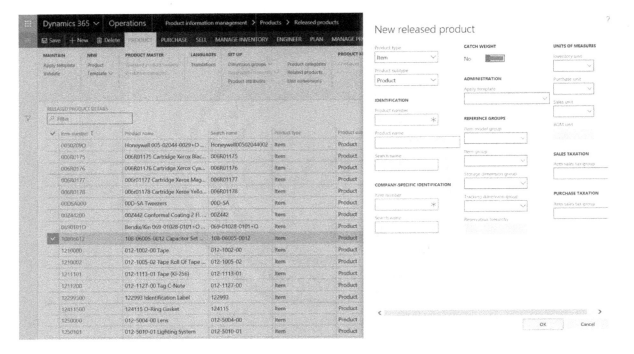

Step 1: Open the Released products form and click New

This will open up the **New released product** panel where we can start specifying our products initial details.

www.dynamicscompanions.com
Dynamics Companions

- 122 -

www.blindsquirrelpublishing.com
© 2019 Blind Squirrel Publishing, LLC , All Rights Reserved

BLIND SQUIRREL
PUBLISHING

DYNAMICS COMPANIONS
BARE BONES CONFIGURATION GUIDE

CONFIGURING PRODUCT INFORMATION MANAGEMENT WITHIN DYNAMICS 365 FOR FINANCE & OPERATIONS
MODULE 2: CONFIGURING PRODUCTS & SERVICES

Creating New Products Using Product Templates

How to do it...

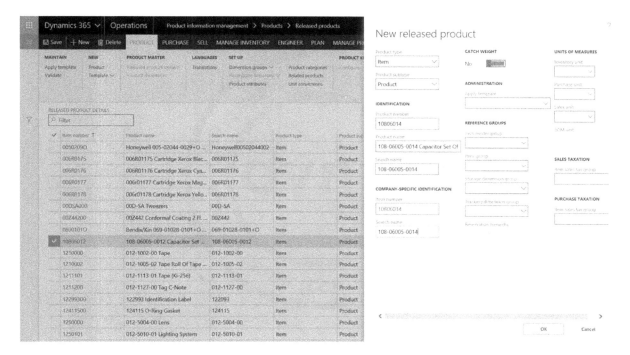

Step 2: Set the Product number Product name and Search name

We will now want to start adding the default codes and descriptions for our new product.

Then the **New Released Product** dialog box is displayed, type in the **Product Number**, the **Product Name**, and set the **Search Names**.

For this example we will set the Product number to 10806014, the Product name to 108-06005-0014 Capacitor Set of 4 Ea and the Search name to 108-06005-0014.

www.dynamicscompanions.com
Dynamics Companions

- 123 -

www.blindsquirrelpublishing.com
© 2019 Blind Squirrel Publishing, LLC , All Rights Reserved

BLIND SQUIRREL
PUBLISHING

DYNAMICS COMPANIONS
BARE BONES CONFIGURATION GUIDE

CONFIGURING PRODUCT INFORMATION MANAGEMENT WITHIN DYNAMICS 365 FOR FINANCE & OPERATIONS
MODULE 2: CONFIGURING PRODUCTS & SERVICES

Creating New Products Using Product Templates

How to do it...

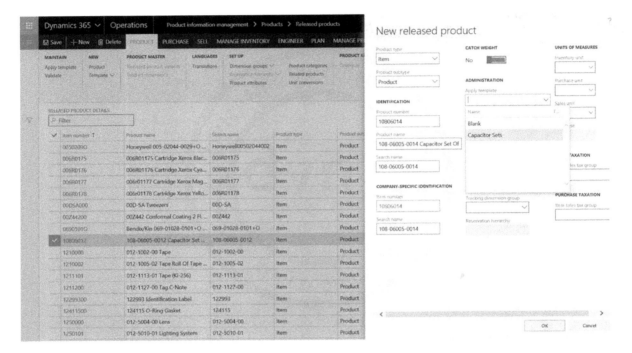

Step 3: Select the Apply template

You will notice that something is a little different now that you have the templates created, there is a new field group called **Administration** with a new **Apply template** field.

Now we will want to use one of the templates that we have saved away to default in some more information on the product.

To do this we will just need to select the **Apply template** from the dropdown list.

For this example, we will want to click on the **Apply template** dropdown list and select **Capacitor Sets**.

dyn c
www.dynamicscompanions.com
Dynamics Companions

- 124 -

www.blindsquirrelpublishing.com
© 2019 Blind Squirrel Publishing, LLC , All Rights Reserved

BLIND SQUIRREL
PUBLISHING

DYNAMICS COMPANIONS
BARE BONES CONFIGURATION GUIDE

CONFIGURING PRODUCT INFORMATION MANAGEMENT WITHIN DYNAMICS 365 FOR FINANCE & OPERATIONS
MODULE 2: CONFIGURING PRODUCTS & SERVICES

Creating New Products Using Product Templates

How to do it...

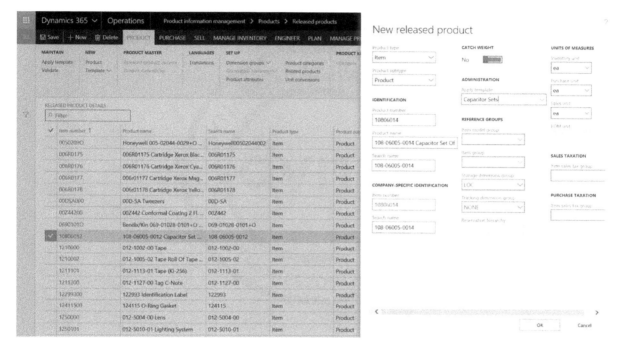

Step 4: Click OK

This will default in all of the codes that you had configured on the master record for you into this new record.

If everything looks good then we can create the new record.

To do this just click on the **OK** button.

www.dynamicscompanions.com
Dynamics Companions

- 125 -

www.blindsquirrelpublishing.com
© 2019 Blind Squirrel Publishing, LLC, All Rights Reserved

BLIND SQUIRREL
PUBLISHING

DYNAMICS COMPANIONS
BARE BONES CONFIGURATION GUIDE

CONFIGURING PRODUCT INFORMATION MANAGEMENT WITHIN DYNAMICS 365 FOR FINANCE & OPERATIONS
MODULE 2: CONFIGURING PRODUCTS & SERVICES

Creating New Products Using Product Templates

How to do it...

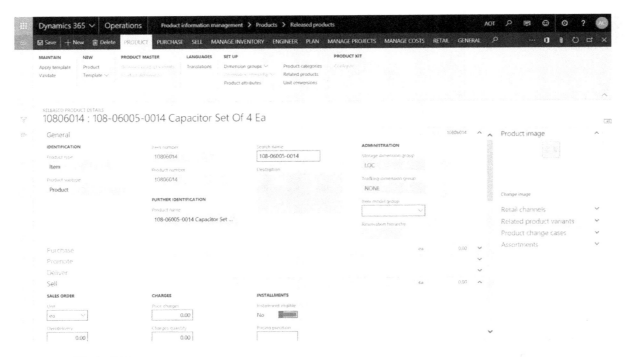

Step 4: Click OK

When we return back to the product that we just created we will see that not only have the units been updated, but also the default pricing and any other fields that you may have configured.

This is a great way to quickly set up common products.

www.dynamicscompanions.com
Dynamics Companions

- 126 -

www.blindsquirrelpublishing.com
© 2019 Blind Squirrel Publishing, LLC , All Rights Reserved

BLIND SQUIRREL
PUBLISHING

DYNAMICS COMPANIONS
BARE BONES CONFIGURATION GUIDE

CONFIGURING PRODUCT INFORMATION MANAGEMENT WITHIN DYNAMICS 365 FOR FINANCE & OPERATIONS
MODULE 2: CONFIGURING PRODUCTS & SERVICES

Applying Templates In Bulk to Multiple Records

To make this even more useful, you can also use the templates on records that already have already been created allowing you to perform mass updates on your products if you like.

How to do it...

Step 1: Click Apply template

Now we will want to apply the template that we created to a number of products at once.

Select the products and click on the **Apply template** button.

Step 2: Select the template and click OK

This will open up a new dialog box that will show us all of the templates that we have created that we can apply to the products.

All we need to do is select the template.

Select the template and click on the **OK** button.

When you return the products will be updated and we can drill into any of the products if you don't believe us.

DYNAMICS COMPANIONS
BARE BONES CONFIGURATION GUIDE

CONFIGURING PRODUCT INFORMATION MANAGEMENT WITHIN DYNAMICS 365 FOR FINANCE & OPERATIONS
MODULE 2: CONFIGURING PRODUCTS & SERVICES

Applying Templates In Bulk to Multiple Records

How to do it...

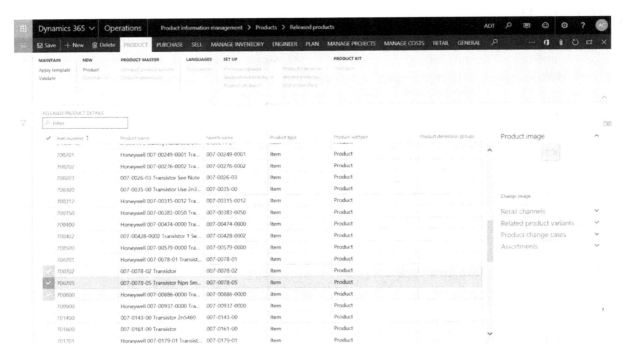

Step 1: Click Apply template

Now we will want to apply the template that we created to a number of products at once.

To do this, just select the products that we want to apply the template to and then click on the **Apply Template** button within the **Maintain** group of the **Product** ribbon bar.

DYNAMICS COMPANIONS
BARE BONES CONFIGURATION GUIDE

CONFIGURING PRODUCT INFORMATION MANAGEMENT WITHIN DYNAMICS 365 FOR FINANCE & OPERATIONS
MODULE 2: CONFIGURING PRODUCTS & SERVICES

Applying Templates In Bulk to Multiple Records

How to do it...

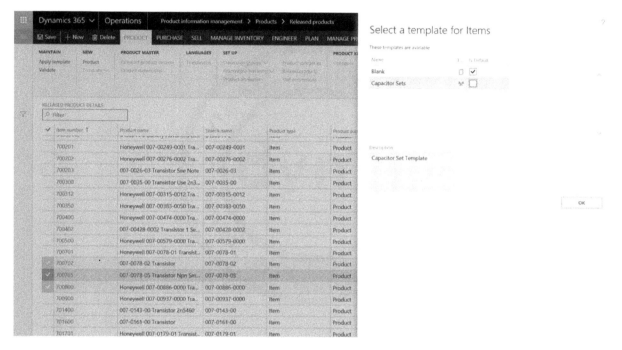

Step 2: Select the template and click OK

This will open up a new dialog box that will show us all of the templates that we have created that we can apply to the products.

All we need to do is select the template.

To do this just select the template that we want to apply and click on the **OK** button.

For this example we selected the **Capacitor Sets** template.

dyne
www.dynamicscompanions.com
Dynamics Companions

- 129 -

www.blindsquirrelpublishing.com
© 2019 Blind Squirrel Publishing, LLC, All Rights Reserved

BLIND SQUIRREL
PUBLISHING

DYNAMICS COMPANIONS
BARE BONES CONFIGURATION GUIDE

CONFIGURING PRODUCT INFORMATION MANAGEMENT WITHIN DYNAMICS 365 FOR FINANCE & OPERATIONS
MODULE 2: CONFIGURING PRODUCTS & SERVICES

Applying Templates In Bulk to Multiple Records

How to do it...

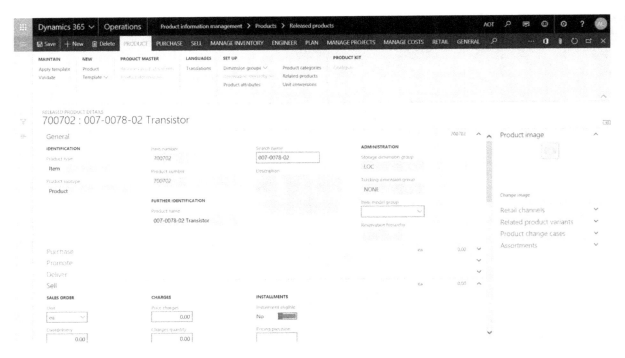

Step 2: Select the template and click OK

When you return the products will be updated and we can drill into any of the products if you don't believe us.

www.dynamicscompanions.com
Dynamics Companions

- 130 -

www.blindsquirrelpublishing.com
© 2019 Blind Squirrel Publishing, LLC , All Rights Reserved

BLIND SQUIRREL
PUBLISHING

DYNAMICS COMPANIONS
BARE BONES CONFIGURATION GUIDE

CONFIGURING PRODUCT INFORMATION MANAGEMENT WITHIN DYNAMICS 365 FOR FINANCE & OPERATIONS
MODULE 2: CONFIGURING PRODUCTS & SERVICES

Updating Product Details Using The Edit In Grid Function

If you want to perform mass updates of your products, or just want an easy way to look at all of your products and make slight tweaks to them, then you can use the **Grid Edit** feature. This allows you to update the records as if they were a spreadsheet. You can make it even more useful by using the **Personalization** option to add additional fields that you may want to update – even if they are not on the main product table itself.

How to do it...

Step 1: Open the Released Products form through the menu

To start off we will open up the **Released products** list page

Navigate to Product information management > Products > Released Products

Step 2: Click Edit

Now we will want to switch the list page from read mode to grid edit mode.

Click on the **Edit** button.

Step 3: Click Hide Fact Boxes Icon

Also, if the **Fact boxes** are showing up on the right hand side of the form, then we may want to hide them so that we can get more real-estate.

Click on the **Hide Fact Boxes Icon** button.

Step 4: Click Personalize

Now we will want to add some more fields to the list page so that we can update more information on each of the products.

Right-mouse-click on the form and select the **Personalize** option.

Step 5: Click Personalize this form

This will open up the **Personalize** options for whichever field you choose.

This is the option that will allow us to personalize existing fields, but we want to be able to personalize the whole form.

Click on the **Personalize this form** button.

Step 6: Click +

That will open a new toolbar for the personalization.

Now we want to add some additional fields to the list page.

Click on the **+** button.

Step 7: Select the List

Now we just need to select the list form that we want to add the fields to.

Select the **List Grid**

DYNAMICS COMPANIONS
BARE BONES CONFIGURATION GUIDE

CONFIGURING PRODUCT INFORMATION MANAGEMENT WITHIN DYNAMICS 365 FOR FINANCE & OPERATIONS
MODULE 2: CONFIGURING PRODUCTS & SERVICES

This will open up a **Add a field** panel showing you all of the fields that we can add to the grid.

Step 8: Check the BOM unit field

Now we will want to add some more fields to the grid.

When we return back to the list page we will see that the new field has been added to the form.

Step 9: Add the Buyer Group, Calculation Group, Cost Group, Coverage Group, Product Group, and Product Model Group fields

We can add some more fields to the list page as well to allow us to change more of the product details within the grid.

Check the Buyer Group, Calculation Group, Cost Group, Coverage Group, Product Group, and Product Model Group fields and click Insert

When we return back to the form we will see that the new fields have been added to the form for us.

Step 10: Add the Inventory module parameters Price and Unit fields

We can continue on and add a few more fields to the form. We will start by adding the price fields for the product so that we can quickly adjust the product prices. And we will start by selecting the purchase price fields.

Add the Inventory module parameters Price and Unit fields

Step 11: Add the second Inventory module parameters Price and Unit fields

And we will continue by selecting the inventory cost fields.

Add the second Inventory module parameters Price and Unit fields

Step 12: Add the third Inventory module parameters Price and Unit fields

Finally we will want to add the sales price unit and value.

Add the third Inventory module parameters Price and Unit fields

Step 13: Click Close

When we return back to list page we will now see that the price information is displayed on the form.

Now we can exit from the personalization mode and return back to the list page.

Click on the **Close** button.

Now you will see a lot more data that you can start tweaking.

If you scroll over to the right then you will also see all of the Price and Cost details are there ready for you to edit within the grid.

dyn
www.dynamicscompanions.com
Dynamics Companions

- 132 -

www.blindsquirrelpublishing.com
© 2019 Blind Squirrel Publishing, LLC , All Rights Reserved

BLIND SQUIRREL
PUBLISHING

DYNAMICS COMPANIONS
BARE BONES CONFIGURATION GUIDE

CONFIGURING PRODUCT INFORMATION MANAGEMENT WITHIN DYNAMICS 365 FOR FINANCE & OPERATIONS
MODULE 2: CONFIGURING PRODUCTS & SERVICES

Updating Product Details Using The Edit In Grid Function

How to do it...

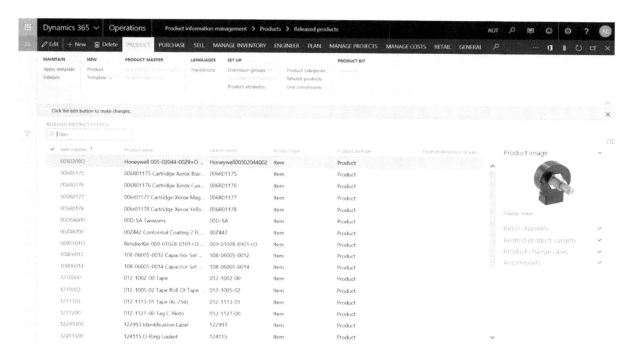

Step 1: Open the Released Products form through the menu

To start off we will open up the **Released products** list page

To do this, open up the navigation panel, expand out the **Modules** and group, and click on **Product information management** to see all of the menu items that are available. Then click on the **Released Products** menu item within the **Products** group.

dync   www.dynamicscompanions.com
Dynamics Companions

- 133 -

www.blindsquirrelpublishing.com
© 2019 Blind Squirrel Publishing, LLC, All Rights Reserved

BLIND SQUIRREL
PUBLISHING

DYNAMICS COMPANIONS
BARE BONES CONFIGURATION GUIDE

CONFIGURING PRODUCT INFORMATION MANAGEMENT WITHIN DYNAMICS 365 FOR FINANCE & OPERATIONS
MODULE 2: CONFIGURING PRODUCTS & SERVICES

Updating Product Details Using The Edit In Grid Function

How to do it...

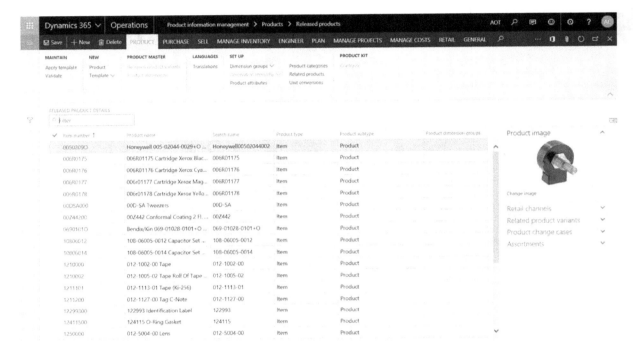

Step 2: Click Edit

Now we will want to switch the list page from read mode to grid edit mode.

To do this just click on the **Edit** button in the menu bar.

www.dynamicscompanions.com
Dynamics Companions

- 134 -

www.blindsquirrelpublishing.com
© 2019 Blind Squirrel Publishing, LLC , All Rights Reserved

BLIND SQUIRREL
PUBLISHING

DYNAMICS COMPANIONS
BARE BONES CONFIGURATION GUIDE

CONFIGURING PRODUCT INFORMATION MANAGEMENT WITHIN DYNAMICS 365 FOR FINANCE & OPERATIONS
MODULE 2: CONFIGURING PRODUCTS & SERVICES

Updating Product Details Using The Edit In Grid Function

How to do it...

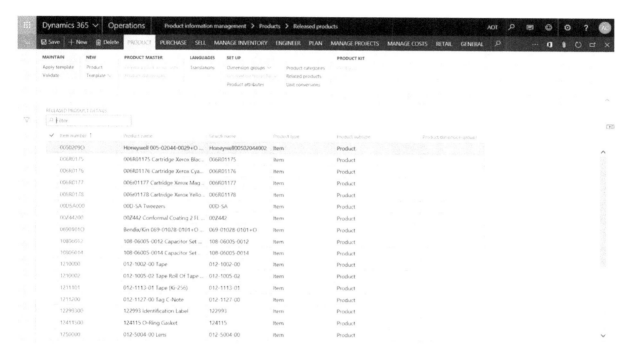

Step 3: Click Hide Fact Boxes Icon

Also, if the **Fact boxes** are showing up on the right hand side of the form, then we may want to hide them so that we can get more real-estate.

To do this just click on the **Hide Fact Boxes Icon** button beside the fact boxes.

This will hide them so that you just see the grid information.

www.dynamicscompanions.com
Dynamics Companions

- 135 -

www.blindsquirrelpublishing.com
© 2019 Blind Squirrel Publishing, LLC , All Rights Reserved

BLIND SQUIRREL
PUBLISHING

DYNAMICS COMPANIONS
BARE BONES CONFIGURATION GUIDE

CONFIGURING PRODUCT INFORMATION MANAGEMENT WITHIN DYNAMICS 365 FOR FINANCE & OPERATIONS
MODULE 2: CONFIGURING PRODUCTS & SERVICES

Updating Product Details Using The Edit In Grid Function

How to do it...

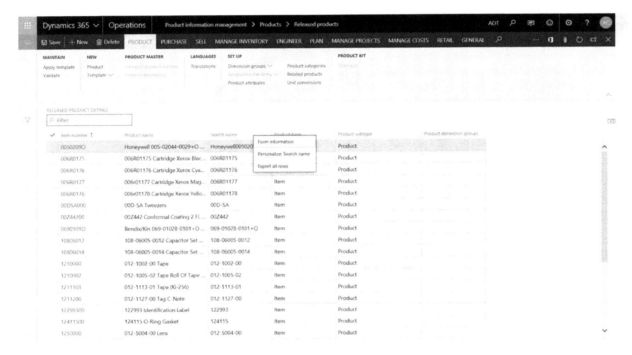

Step 4: Click Personalize

Now we will want to add some more fields to the list page so that we can update more information on each of the products.

To do this we just need to right-mouse-click anywhere on the form and select the **Personalize** menu item from the context menu.

www.dynamicscompanions.com
Dynamics Companions

- 136 -

www.blindsquirrelpublishing.com
© 2019 Blind Squirrel Publishing, LLC , All Rights Reserved

BLIND SQUIRREL
PUBLISHING

DYNAMICS COMPANIONS
BARE BONES CONFIGURATION GUIDE

CONFIGURING PRODUCT INFORMATION MANAGEMENT WITHIN DYNAMICS 365 FOR FINANCE & OPERATIONS
MODULE 2: CONFIGURING PRODUCTS & SERVICES

Updating Product Details Using The Edit In Grid Function

How to do it...

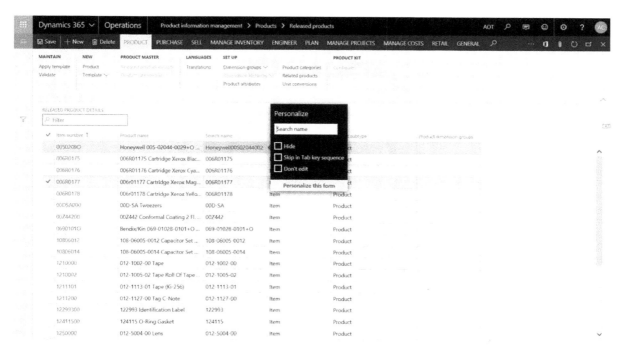

Step 5: Click Personalize this form

This will open up the **Personalize** options for whichever field you choose.

This is the option that will allow us to personalize existing fields, but we want to be able to personalize the whole form.

To do this just click on the **Personalize this form** button.

dync
www.dynamicscompanions.com
Dynamics Companions

- 137 -

www.blindsquirrelpublishing.com
© 2019 Blind Squirrel Publishing, LLC , All Rights Reserved

BLIND SQUIRREL
PUBLISHING

DYNAMICS COMPANIONS
BARE BONES CONFIGURATION GUIDE

CONFIGURING PRODUCT INFORMATION MANAGEMENT WITHIN DYNAMICS 365 FOR FINANCE & OPERATIONS
MODULE 2: CONFIGURING PRODUCTS & SERVICES

Updating Product Details Using The Edit In Grid Function

How to do it...

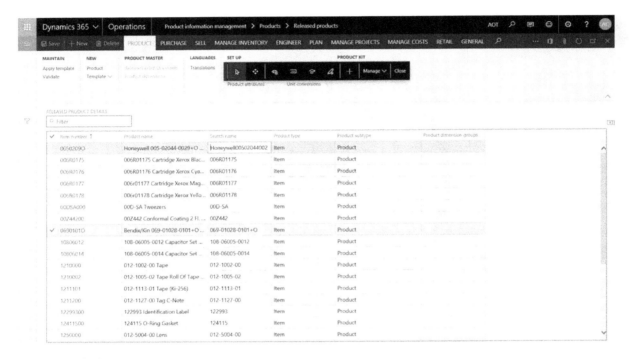

Step 6: Click +

That will open a new toolbar for the personalization.

Now we want to add some additional fields to the list page.

To do this just click on the **+** button.

www.dynamicscompanions.com
Dynamics Companions

- 138 -

www.blindsquirrelpublishing.com
© 2019 Blind Squirrel Publishing, LLC , All Rights Reserved

BLIND SQUIRREL
PUBLISHING

DYNAMICS COMPANIONS
BARE BONES CONFIGURATION GUIDE

CONFIGURING PRODUCT INFORMATION MANAGEMENT WITHIN DYNAMICS 365 FOR FINANCE & OPERATIONS
MODULE 2: CONFIGURING PRODUCTS & SERVICES

Updating Product Details Using The Edit In Grid Function

How to do it...

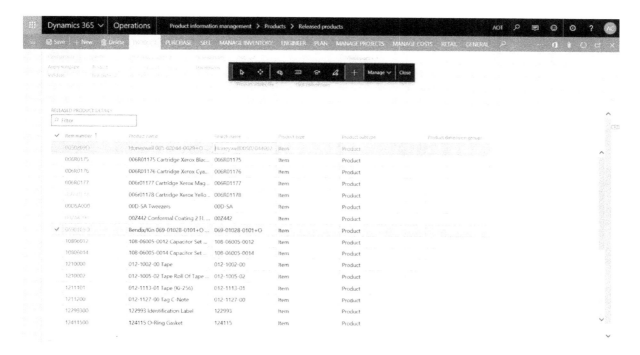

Step 7: Select the List

Now we just need to select the list form that we want to add the fields to.

To do this we just need to click on the list grid control.

www.dynamicscompanions.com
Dynamics Companions

- 139 -

www.blindsquirrelpublishing.com
© 2019 Blind Squirrel Publishing, LLC , All Rights Reserved

BLIND SQUIRREL
PUBLISHING

DYNAMICS COMPANIONS
BARE BONES CONFIGURATION GUIDE

CONFIGURING PRODUCT INFORMATION MANAGEMENT WITHIN DYNAMICS 365 FOR FINANCE & OPERATIONS
MODULE 2: CONFIGURING PRODUCTS & SERVICES

Updating Product Details Using The Edit In Grid Function

How to do it...

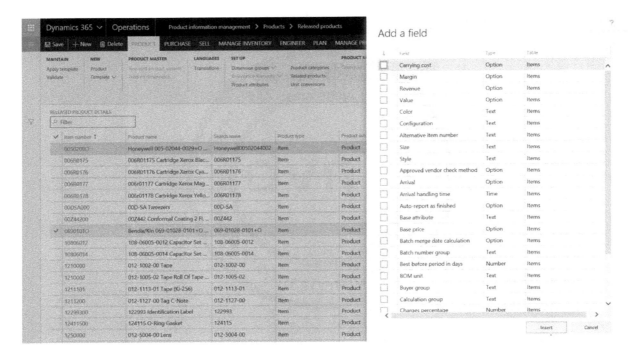

Step 7: Select the List

This will open up a **Add a field** panel showing you all of the fields that we can add to the grid.

DYNAMICS COMPANIONS
BARE BONES CONFIGURATION GUIDE

CONFIGURING PRODUCT INFORMATION MANAGEMENT WITHIN DYNAMICS 365 FOR FINANCE & OPERATIONS
MODULE 2: CONFIGURING PRODUCTS & SERVICES

Updating Product Details Using The Edit In Grid Function

How to do it...

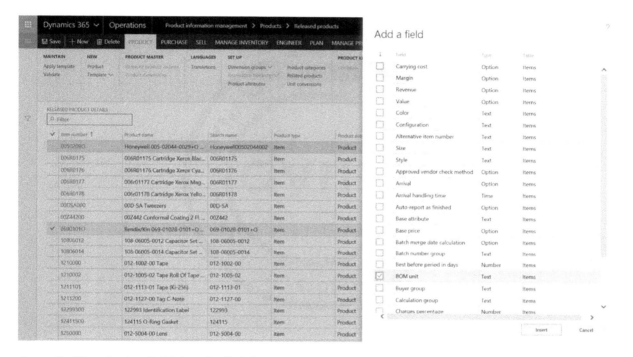

Step 8: Check the BOM unit field

Now we will want to add some more fields to the grid.

To do that, all you need to do is find the field that you want to add and then check the checkbox, and when we have selected the fields, just click on the **insert** button.

In this example we will check the **BOM unit** field and then click on the **Insert** button.

www.dynamicscompanions.com
Dynamics Companions

- 141 -

www.blindsquirrelpublishing.com
© 2019 Blind Squirrel Publishing, LLC , All Rights Reserved

BLIND SQUIRREL
PUBLISHING

DYNAMICS COMPANIONS
BARE BONES CONFIGURATION GUIDE

CONFIGURING PRODUCT INFORMATION MANAGEMENT WITHIN DYNAMICS 365 FOR FINANCE & OPERATIONS
MODULE 2: CONFIGURING PRODUCTS & SERVICES

Updating Product Details Using The Edit In Grid Function

How to do it...

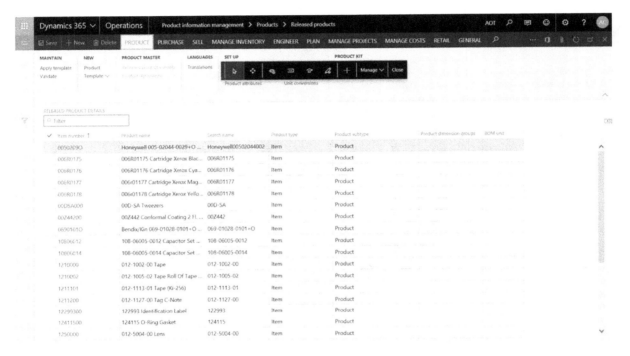

Step 8: Check the BOM unit field

When we return back to the list page we will see that the new field has been added to the form.

DYNAMICS COMPANIONS
BARE BONES CONFIGURATION GUIDE

CONFIGURING PRODUCT INFORMATION MANAGEMENT WITHIN DYNAMICS 365 FOR FINANCE & OPERATIONS
MODULE 2: CONFIGURING PRODUCTS & SERVICES

Updating Product Details Using The Edit In Grid Function

How to do it...

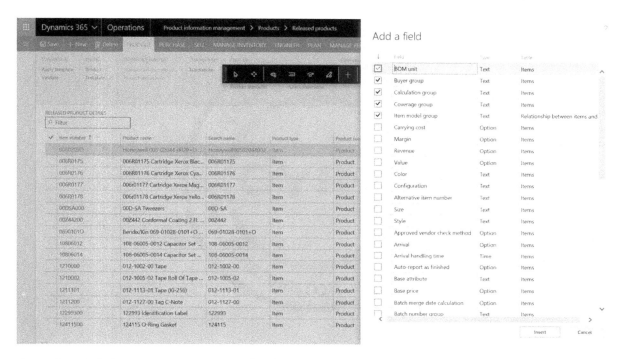

Step 9: Add the Buyer Group, Calculation Group, Cost Group, Coverage Group, Product Group, and Product Model Group fields

All we need to do is open up the **Add a field** panel, select the fields that you want to add to the form and then click on the **Insert** button.

For this example we will select the Buyer Group, Calculation Group, Cost Group, Coverage Group, Product Group, and Product Model Group fields from the list.

www.dynamicscompanions.com
Dynamics Companions

- 143 -

www.blindsquirrelpublishing.com
© 2019 Blind Squirrel Publishing, LLC , All Rights Reserved

BLIND SQUIRREL
PUBLISHING

DYNAMICS COMPANIONS
BARE BONES CONFIGURATION GUIDE

CONFIGURING PRODUCT INFORMATION MANAGEMENT WITHIN DYNAMICS 365 FOR FINANCE & OPERATIONS
MODULE 2: CONFIGURING PRODUCTS & SERVICES

Updating Product Details Using The Edit In Grid Function

How to do it...

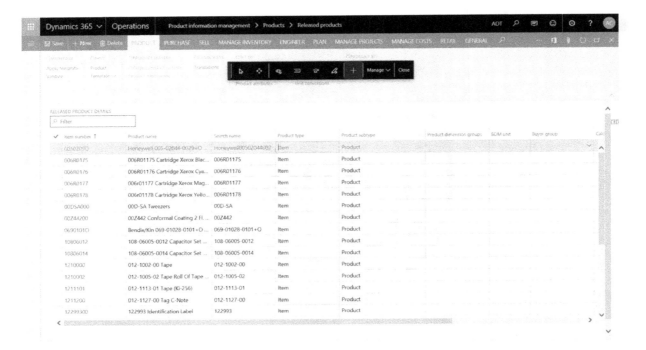

Step 9: Add the Buyer Group, Calculation Group, Cost Group, Coverage Group, Product Group, and Product Model Group fields

When we return back to the form we will see that the new fields have been added to the form for us.

www.dynamicscompanions.com
Dynamics Companions

- 144 -

www.blindsquirrelpublishing.com
© 2019 Blind Squirrel Publishing, LLC , All Rights Reserved

BLIND SQUIRREL
PUBLISHING

DYNAMICS COMPANIONS
BARE BONES CONFIGURATION GUIDE

CONFIGURING PRODUCT INFORMATION MANAGEMENT WITHIN DYNAMICS 365 FOR FINANCE & OPERATIONS
MODULE 2: CONFIGURING PRODUCTS & SERVICES

Updating Product Details Using The Edit In Grid Function

How to do it...

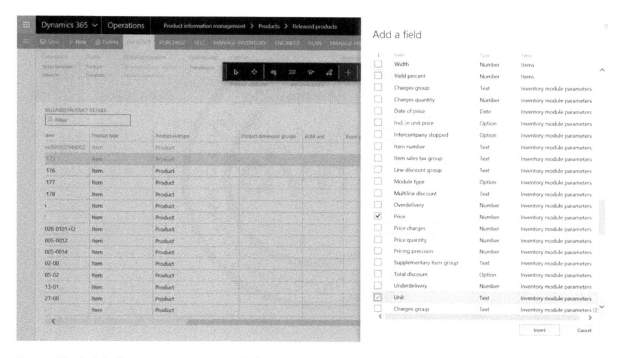

Step 10: Add the Inventory module parameters Price and Unit fields

All we need to do is open up the **Add a field** panel, select the fields that you want to add to the form and then click on the **Insert** button.

For this example we will want to find the **Inventory Module Parameters** fields and select the **Price** and **Unit** fields.

dyn c   www.dynamicscompanions.com
Dynamics Companions

- 145 -

www.blindsquirrelpublishing.com
© 2019 Blind Squirrel Publishing, LLC , All Rights Reserved

BLIND SQUIRREL
PUBLISHING

DYNAMICS COMPANIONS
BARE BONES CONFIGURATION GUIDE

CONFIGURING PRODUCT INFORMATION MANAGEMENT WITHIN DYNAMICS 365 FOR FINANCE & OPERATIONS
MODULE 2: CONFIGURING PRODUCTS & SERVICES

Updating Product Details Using The Edit In Grid Function

How to do it...

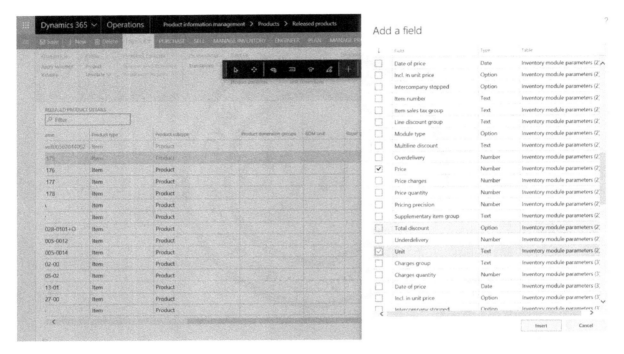

Step 11: Add the second Inventory module parameters Price and Unit fields

And we will continue by selecting the inventory cost fields.

All we need to do is open up the **Add a field** panel, select the fields that you want to add to the form and then click on the **Insert** button.

For this example we will want to find the second group of **Inventory Module Parameters** fields and select the **Price** and **Unit** fields.

www.dynamicscompanions.com
Dynamics Companions

- 146 -

www.blindsquirrelpublishing.com
© 2019 Blind Squirrel Publishing, LLC , All Rights Reserved

BLIND SQUIRREL
PUBLISHING

DYNAMICS COMPANIONS
BARE BONES CONFIGURATION GUIDE

CONFIGURING PRODUCT INFORMATION MANAGEMENT WITHIN DYNAMICS 365 FOR FINANCE & OPERATIONS
MODULE 2: CONFIGURING PRODUCTS & SERVICES

Updating Product Details Using The Edit In Grid Function

How to do it...

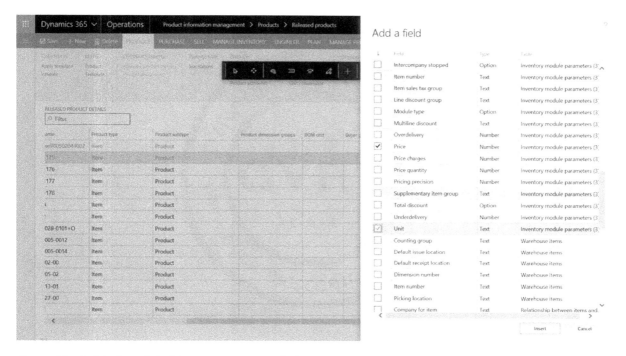

Step 12: Add the third Inventory module parameters Price and Unit fields

Finally we will want to add the sales price unit and value.

All we need to do is open up the **Add a field** panel, select the fields that you want to add to the form and then click on the **Insert** button.

For this example we will want to find the third group of **Inventory Module Parameters** fields and select the **Price** and **Unit** fields.

dyn

www.dynamicscompanions.com
Dynamics Companions

- 147 -

www.blindsquirrelpublishing.com
© 2019 Blind Squirrel Publishing, LLC , All Rights Reserved

BLIND SQUIRREL
PUBLISHING

DYNAMICS COMPANIONS
BARE BONES CONFIGURATION GUIDE

CONFIGURING PRODUCT INFORMATION MANAGEMENT WITHIN DYNAMICS 365 FOR FINANCE & OPERATIONS
MODULE 2: CONFIGURING PRODUCTS & SERVICES

Updating Product Details Using The Edit In Grid Function

How to do it...

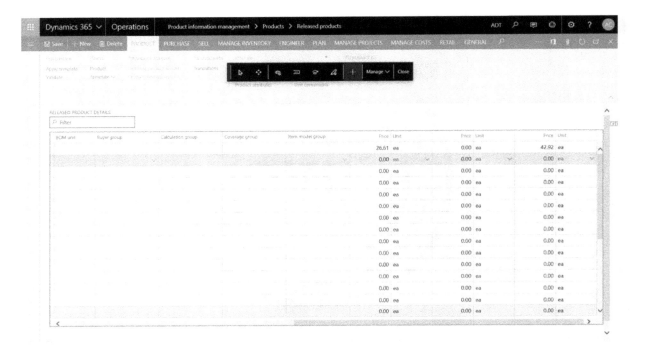

Step 13: Click Close

When we return back to list page we will now see that the price information is displayed on the form.

Now we can exit from the personalization mode and return back to the list page.

To do this just click on the **Close** button.

www.dynamicscompanions.com
Dynamics Companions

- 148 -

www.blindsquirrelpublishing.com
© 2019 Blind Squirrel Publishing, LLC , All Rights Reserved

BLIND SQUIRREL
PUBLISHING

DYNAMICS COMPANIONS
BARE BONES CONFIGURATION GUIDE

CONFIGURING PRODUCT INFORMATION MANAGEMENT WITHIN DYNAMICS 365 FOR FINANCE & OPERATIONS
MODULE 2: CONFIGURING PRODUCTS & SERVICES

Updating Product Details Using The Edit In Grid Function

How to do it...

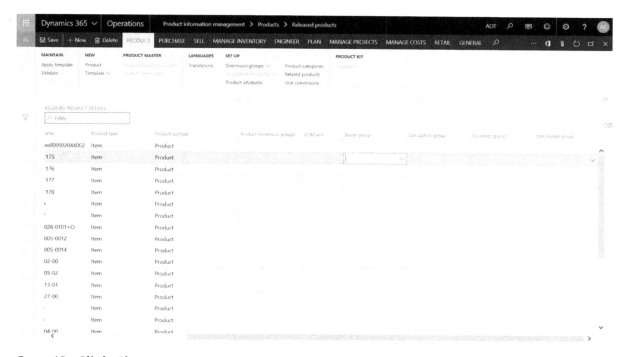

Step 13: Click Close

Now you will see a lot more data that you can start tweaking.

dyn c

www.dynamicscompanions.com
Dynamics Companions

- 149 -

www.blindsquirrelpublishing.com
© 2019 Blind Squirrel Publishing, LLC , All Rights Reserved

BLIND SQUIRREL
PUBLISHING

DYNAMICS COMPANIONS
BARE BONES CONFIGURATION GUIDE

CONFIGURING PRODUCT INFORMATION MANAGEMENT WITHIN DYNAMICS 365 FOR FINANCE & OPERATIONS
MODULE 2: CONFIGURING PRODUCTS & SERVICES

Updating Product Details Using The Edit In Grid Function

How to do it...

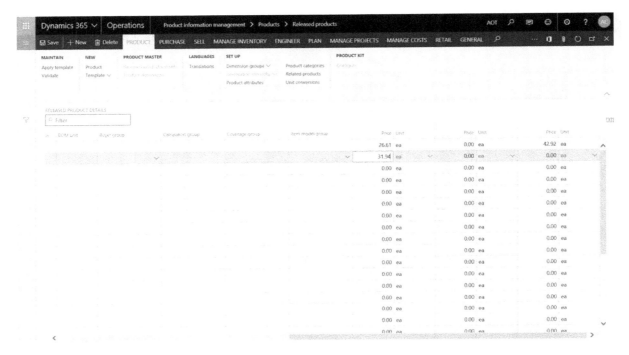

Step 13: Click Close

If you scroll over to the right then you will also see all of the Price and Cost details are there ready for you to edit within the grid.

DYNAMICS COMPANIONS
BARE BONES CONFIGURATION GUIDE

CONFIGURING PRODUCT INFORMATION MANAGEMENT WITHIN DYNAMICS 365 FOR FINANCE & OPERATIONS
MODULE 2: CONFIGURING PRODUCTS & SERVICES

Summary

In this section we have shown you some of the other ways that you can update your product records to make your life a little but easier. Templates are a great way to create your products based off other product configurations, and the Edit in grid feature is a lifesaver when it comes to making a lot of similar changes to groups of products.

DYNAMICS COMPANIONS
BARE BONES CONFIGURATION GUIDE

CONFIGURING PRODUCT INFORMATION MANAGEMENT WITHIN DYNAMICS 365 FOR FINANCE & OPERATIONS
MODULE 2: CONFIGURING PRODUCTS & SERVICES

Review

Congratulations. You now know how to configure Products and Services within Dynamics 365, and along the way we have also looked at a couple of different ways to update the products and templatize them as well.

How east was that?

DYNAMICS COMPANIONS
BARE BONES CONFIGURATION GUIDE

CONFIGURING PRODUCT INFORMATION MANAGEMENT WITHIN DYNAMICS 365 FOR FINANCE & OPERATIONS
MODULE 2: CONFIGURING PRODUCTS & SERVICES

About The Author

Murray Fife is an Author of over 20 books on Microsoft Dynamics including the Bare Bones Configuration Guide series. These guides comprise of over 15 books which step you through the setup and configuration of Microsoft Dynamics including Finance, Operations, Human Resources, Production, Service Management, and Project Accounting.

Throughout his 25+ years of experience in the software industry he has worked in many different roles during his career, including as a developer, an implementation consultant, a trainer and a demo guy within the partner channel which gives him a great understanding of the requirements for both customers and partners perspective.

If you are interested in contacting Murray or want to follow his blogs and posts then here is all of his contact information:

Email:	murray@murrayfife.com
Twitter:	@murrayfife
Facebook:	facebook.com/murraycfife
Google:	google.com/+murrayfife
LinkedIn:	linkedin.com/in/murrayfife
Blog:	atinkerersnotebook.com
Slideshare:	slideshare.net/murrayfife
Amazon:	amazon.com/author/murrayfife

 www.dynamicscompanions.com
Dynamics Companions

- 153 -

www.blindsquirrelpublishing.com
© 2019 Blind Squirrel Publishing, LLC , All Rights Reserved

BLIND SQUIRREL
PUBLISHING

DYNAMICS COMPANIONS
BARE BONES CONFIGURATION GUIDE

CONFIGURING PRODUCT INFORMATION MANAGEMENT WITHIN DYNAMICS 365 FOR FINANCE & OPERATIONS
MODULE 2: CONFIGURING PRODUCTS & SERVICES

Need More Help with Microsoft Dynamics AX 2012 or Dynamics 365 for Operations

We are firm believers that Microsoft Dynamics AX 2012 or Dynamics 365 is not a hard product to learn, but the problem is where do you start. Which is why we developed the Bare Bones Configuration Guides. The aim of this series is to step you though the configuration of Microsoft Dynamics from a blank system, and then step you through the setup of all of the core modules within Microsoft Dynamics. We start with the setup of a base system, then move on to the financial, distribution, and operations modules.

Each book builds upon the previous ones, and by the time you have worked through all of the guides then you will have completely configured a simple (but functional) Microsoft Dynamics instance. To make it even more worthwhile you will have a far better understanding of Microsoft Dynamics and also how everything fits together.

As of now there are 16 guides in this series broken out as follows:

- Configuring a Training Environment

- Configuring an Organization

- Configuring the General Ledger

- Configuring Cash and Bank Management

- Configuring Accounts Receivable

- Configuring Accounts Payable

- Configuring Product Information Management

- Configuring Inventory Management

- Configuring Procurement and Sourcing

- Configuring Sales Order Management

- Configuring Human Resource Management

- Configuring Project Management and Accounting

- Configuring Production Control

- Configuring Sales and Marketing

- Configuring Service Management

- Configuring Warehouse Management

Although you can get each of these guides individually, and we think that each one is a great Visual resources to step you through each of the particular modules, for those of you that want to take full advantage of the series, you will want to start from the beginning and work through them one by one. After you have done that you would have done people told me was impossible for one persons to do, and that is to configure all of the core modules within Microsoft Dynamics.

If you are interested in finding out more about the series and also view all of the details including topics covered within the module, then browse to the Bare Bones Configuration Guide landing page on the Microsoft Dynamics Companions website. You will find all of the details, and also downloadable resources that help you with the setup of Microsoft Dynamics. Here is the full link: http://www.dynamicscompanions.com/

www.dynamicscompanions.com
Dynamics Companions

- 155 -

www.blindsquirrelpublishing.com
© 2019 Blind Squirrel Publishing, LLC , All Rights Reserved

BLIND SQUIRREL
PUBLISHING